The Yorkshire Country House

Peter Tuffrey

GREAT NORTHERN

ACKNOWLEDGEMENTS

I am grateful for the assistance received from the following people: Roger Arnold; David Burrill; David Clay; Jeremy Clifford; Simon Cunliffe-Lister; Ian Day; Mike Gosling; David Joy; Nick Lane Fox; Hugh Parkin

Special thanks are due to my son Tristram for his help and encouragement throughout the project.

PHOTOGRAPHS

Pictures marked YP are from the *Yorkshire Post* archives and reproduced courtesy of Yorkshire Post Newspapers.

INFORMATION

I have taken reasonable steps to verify the accuracy of the information in this book but it may contain errors or omissions. Any information that may be of assistance to rectify any problems will be gratefully received. Please contact me by email petertuffrey@rocketmail.com or in writing: Peter Tuffrey, 8 Wrightson Avenue, Warmsworth, Doncaster, South Yorkshire, DN4 9QL.

Great Northern Books Limited
PO Box 1380, Bradford, BD5 5FB
www.greatnorthernbooks.co.uk

ISBN: 978-1-912101-67-2

Design and layout: David Burrill

CIP Data
A catalogue for this book is available from the British Library

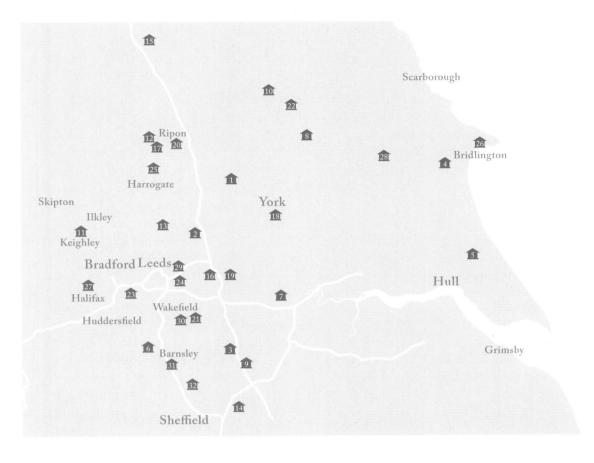

Introduction *by David Joy*

Nowhere else has arguably as much to offer in the way of great country houses as does Yorkshire. They stretch across the traditional boundaries of the county from the slopes of the Pennine dales through the low-lying Vale of York all the way to the coast. Of infinite variety in terms of age and grandeur, they are glorious survivors of a bygone age.

Their origins are frequently extraordinary, perhaps none more so than Castle Howard – regarded as the foremost country house in Yorkshire and among the most spectacular in Britain. The late 17th century saw houses becoming ever more ostentatious, symbolizing their owners' power and social position. It was the age of the Whig nobility, with a select circle gathering at the infamous Kit-Kat Club in London. Among them was Charles Howard, 3rd Earl of Carlisle, who invited a playwright John Vanbrugh, noted for his wit and bawdy plays, to join them. Even though he had no previous architectural experience, Vanbrugh was duly asked to design Castle Howard. It was a bizarre but brilliantly successful commission and he went on to create his masterpiece at Blenheim Palace. Small wonder that he had a celebrated epigram: 'Lie heavy on him, Earth, for he laid many a heavy load on thee.'

Today the house is part of an estate still run by members of the Howard family. It is remarkable how many of the properties featured in these pages remain occupied by the same families that created them centuries ago. They are symbolic of survival and sheer determination, as shown at Burton Constable, Harewood House and Newby Hall. A prime example is Burton Agnes, near Bridlington, where the estate has never changed hands by sale since the Norman manor house was built in 1173. It has simply slid from family to family when the male line has ended, the early years of the 17th century seeing master masons build one of the finest houses in England. This has survived to the present day and is still a lived-in family home, open to the public in the summer months and housing a superb art collection.

Then there is Ripley Castle, north of Harrogate, seat of the Ingilby family who can trace their lineage back almost a thousand years to the time of William the Conqueror. They moved to Ripley in the 13th century and developed a castle that withstood debt and many a disaster as it was gradually transformed from fortress to country house. It too remains a family home but has been open to the public for over 60 years and has become a favourite location for television and film.

There are many other instances of families clinging to their roots with limpet-like determination against setbacks that must have been close to overwhelming. One of the most devastating – and also the most fascinating – was fire. Way back in 1828 a drunken footman knocking over an oil lamp was reputedly the cause of a blaze at Bramham Park so ferocious that it left the property derelict for the next 80 years. Eventually rebuilt, it is now the home of the 10th generation of its creator's Lane Fox family and is run on modern business lines having become famous for both its horse trials and rock festivals.

Extinguishing a fire was often a mission impossible. When a blaze was discovered at Duncombe Park, Helmsley, in 1879, buckets of water were poured onto the flames by a chain of twelve servant girls before it was decided to summon a steam fire-engine from York on a special train! It was too late and the centre of the building was completely gutted. Similarly, at Sledmere House on the Wolds in 1911, pales of water carried by villagers achieved nothing, but at least the fire spread so slowly that it was possible for another human chain to retrieve most of the contents. In both cases, new houses in the same style were constructed by their dedicated owners.

Despite such commitment, it was not long before the world of the country house started to fall apart. The introduction of 'death duty' taxation, followed by hard economic times after World War I, sounded the end of an 'Upstairs, Downstairs' era now portrayed in countless television dramas. No longer could P.G. Wodehouse characters lead a charmed existence in giant mansions with their every whim at the beck and call of innumerable servants. Great houses were deserted, fell into dereliction and then demolished. Once started it was a trend that seemed unstoppable, although there were notable exceptions along the way.

Nothing seemed to cause more dismay than the prospect that some properties might be completely dismantled and then shipped across the Atlantic by an American tycoon. Among those threatened was the medieval Oakwell Hall, Birstall, where protests were made more vociferous because it had provided the inspiration for 'Fieldhead' in Charlotte Brontë's novel *Shirley*. Bought by private individuals in 1928, it was then donated to the local council and became a museum. The concept of local authorities owning country houses had started six years earlier when the magnificent Temple Newsam was gifted to Leeds, and was followed in the mid-1930s by Shibden Hall and Sewerby Hall respectively passing to Halifax and Bridlington.

Yet these developments were mere blips in the relentless march of destruction, which was only made worse when many properties were requisitioned in World War 2 with scant regard for their contents. Then came even more punitive taxation and it seemed that the end of the country house was nigh. Fortunately it became possible for death duties to be mitigated by properties passing to the National Trust, a long-established body originally set up to safeguard land before it also embraced buildings of historic importance. It had already accepted custodianship of East Riddlesden Hall, Keighley, in 1934 and now in the 1950s it became responsible for such buildings as Nunnington Hall in Ryedale and Nostell Priory, near Wakefield, with its priceless Chippendale furniture.

Happily, this last is still occupied by descendants of the family that have lived there since the 19th century. It accords with increasing recognition that saving a building is one thing but it is far better if it can continue to be a home or have some other use that breathes life into its ancient fabric. Thus, Middlethorpe Hall on the outskirts of York was already an hotel when it passed to the National Trust in 2008. Other country houses on the edge of doom have also become hotels, some of international excellence.

Fortunes change, nowhere better shown than by the immense Wentworth Woodhouse near Barnsley with at over 600 feet the longest frontage of any country house in Britain. Owned by the Fitzwilliams, coal kings in this part of Yorkshire, it came to be seen as symbolic of all that was wrong with aristocratic feudalism. Manny Shinwell, Minister of Fuel in a post-war Labour government, was accused of seeking revenge when he permitted open-cast mining virtually up to the front doorway. The Fitzwilliam titles became extinct and hope for this crumbling structure gradually seemed to evaporate, but ironically it was another politician who ultimately came to the rescue. In hard economic times there was both surprise and relief when in 2016 the Chancellor Philip Hammond announced a grant of over £7 million to safeguard what he saw as 'a key piece of northern heritage'.

Like many country houses, it may now seem ridiculously excessive in size and concept. Yet such buildings undoubtedly reflect a remarkable period of architectural and social history by their very existence. The evocative photographs within the pages of this book are testimony to those who lived, loved, laughed and died within rooms often numbered by the hundred. It was a way of life that should never be forgotten.

Beningbrough Hall

John Bourchier (1684-1736) builder of the present Beningbrough Hall. Painting attributed to Jonathan Richardson the Elder. © National Trust

One man's indifference to ribald activity during his early life may have led to Beningbrough Hall celebrating 300 years of existence in 2016.

John Bourchier was only 16 when he inherited the prosperous Beningbrough estates in 1700; he had lost both his parents some five years earlier. At this period many young wealthy men of his generation embarked on a Grand Tour of Europe finding this an excuse for drunken mischief. This was not the case with John when he began his own Grand Tour over an approx. two year period from September 1704.

Adopting a studious air, he thoroughly enjoyed sightseeing in Italy especially in Padua and Rome when viewing Baroque palaces and churches. Acquiring a copy of Domenico de Rossi's newly published *Studio d'Architettura* probably filled him with ideas to rebuild his family home once back in England.

In 1706 he married wealthy Yorkshire heiress Mary Bellwood and the marriage settlement doubtless boosted his funds to erect a splendid new house.

Beningbrough, or 'Benninburg' was recorded in the Domesday Book of 1086 and owned by an individual named Asford. Later, much of the land which now forms Beningbrough was held by the Hospital of St Leonard, a religious organisation run by monks, using large parts of it for arable farming.

Following the Dissolution of the Monasteries in 1539, the Hospital along with the lands were surrendered to King Henry VIII. Within five years the lands were sold to John Bannester.

It is unclear at this period whether there was a monastic house existing when the lands were inherited by John Bannester's nephew Ralph Bourchier at the age of 25 in 1556.

But on his inheritance we do know that Ralph set about building (or maybe remodelling) a timber framed house located some 300 metres south-east of

A painting of the Hall dated 1751 by J. Bouttats and J. Chapman. There is speculation about whether the pedimented service blocks facing each other ever existed. If they did, it is surmised John Bourchier may have had them built at the same time or very soon after the main house but they were pulled down when the existing stable block was built in the late 18th century. © National Trust

the present house. It is surmised this was built of red-brick and on a modest scale fit for the gentry rather than nobility with perhaps approx. six main rooms that were panelled.

The property was handed down through generations of Bourchiers until it came to John Bourchier at the outset of the 18th century and he had great innovative plans to rebuild and change the face of the Beningbrough estate forever.

Unlike a number of other Yorkshire houses, very little is known of the new Beningbrough Hall's building history. We do know John Bourchier employed a York carpenter/architect, William Thornton, to supervise building the house on a very slight rise above the general level of the Ouse and it was completed in 1716.

Thornton worked as a joiner on a number of Yorkshire houses between 1700-1720 in particular at Castle Howard between 1708-1711. Yet, apart from small commissions nothing other than Beningbrough is recorded concerning his architectural work.

Whilst advice on the more Italianate of Beningbrough's features was possibly given by amateur gentleman British architect Thomas Archer, there is a strong supposition that John Bourchier himself strongly influenced the house's overall Baroque design which resembles other grand houses of the period.

Baroque art and architecture developed between the late 17th and 18th centuries and originated in Italy. Baroque characteristics in architecture display

The Great Hall displaying monumental classical grandeur faces north. It is strongly suspected John Bourchier had a hand in its design. © National Trust

extravagant and elaborate decoration, a sense of movement, bold projections, dramatic views and spatial drama.

Beningbrough Hall is built from small red brick, with architectural details in stone. Externally, the house is quite simple but betrays certain Italianate Baroque influences. Amongst these are the paired cornice brackets just below the roof, the vertical strips of stone marking the corners and projections of the facade, and the curious window frame above the entrance door with its curved ears.

Some architectural details found at Beningbrough may be compared with those included in Thomas Archer's designs at Heythorpe House, Oxfordshire and at St Pauls, Deptford. Beningbrough probably took five or six years to complete.

One marvellous feature on the ground floor at

Beningbrough Hall is the monumental Great Hall on the north front. It cuts through two storeys, includes a huge fireplace and massive imposing fluted pilasters. Resembling the classical grandeur of Rome's Baroque palaces, this is probably a result of John Bourchier's many acute observations during his Grand Tour. Designed to impress visitors, the Great Hall also connects many of the ground floor rooms. Wrought ironwork grilles fronting first floor balconies in the Great Hall are perhaps from the hands of Derbyshire master-ironsmith Robert Bakewell (working 1707-1752).

Other noted areas on the ground floor include the Great Staircase Hall where the staircase seemingly hangs unsupported in the air. But each wooden step hides a long iron bar extending into the wall and these act as a support for those climbing or descending the stairs.

The Drawing Room originally comprised two rooms: the State Bedchamber and the Withdrawing Room. The alteration probably occurred during the 1830s. © National Trust

The Great Staircase Hall. © National Trust

Other rooms have changed use over the years and amongst these are the Blue Bedroom, which may have originally been the Common Parlour; the Drawing Room, initially two separate spaces – a bedroom and a withdrawing room; the Dining Room probably known until the mid-19th century as the 'Great Parlour'.

One of the most important rooms on the ground floor was the State Apartment but its original form was lost in later years. Nonetheless, it has been recreated in the intact south east apartment where an 18th century bed is currently on display.

On the first floor John Bourchier may have called the room now known as The Saloon, the Great Dining Room where there would have been staged large parties, county balls, family celebrations and banquets.

The elaborate Italianate room decoration is not plaster moulding but wood carving by William Thornton.

Several highly skilled French Huguenot craftsmen who worked with William Thornton elsewhere, particularly at Wentworth Castle followed him to Beningbrough. Amongst them were wood carver Jonathan Godier (or Goodyear) and another stone and wood-carver Daniel Herve (or Harvey).

Another craftsman associated with Thornton was York plasterer John Bagnall who also worked at other Yorkshire houses.

Beningbrough Hall's builder died in 1736 and the house and estates passed to his son also called John who, along with his wife, featured prominently in York society. Dying in 1759, aged only 49, his only child Mildred died a year later and so Beningbrough

Left: The State Bedchamber and the state bed.
© National Trust

Below: The Saloon, the principal room on the first floor.
© National Trust

was claimed by an uncle, prominent physician 71-year-old Dr Ralph Bourchier.

He agreed to pass his interest in the house and some 7,000 acres to his only daughter Margaret Bourchier. Marrying Giles Earle in 1761, Margaret and her husband were noted as being unconventional and eight years later they left Beningbrough with their young son William to spend some time in Italy and France. In Italy they acquired a bust of the Pope, Clement XIV and artist Piranesi also dedicated to them three plates in a series of etchings.

Much to the amusement of a number of people, Margret returned from France fashionably dressed and with a broken English accent.

The couple seemingly experienced financial troubles in the late 1770s with the estate mortgaged for £12,000, though the crisis eased after the sale of a house they owned at Hendon. During the couple's time at Beningbrough improvements were made to the stables and a new lodge was added at Newton.

Giles Earle died in 1811 and his wife Margaret, the last of the Bourchier line, in October 1827. There was no heir as their two sons were killed in the war against Napoleon.

Margaret left Beningbrough to the Rev. William Henry Dawnay aged 55. He had been a close friend of her elder son at Eton. She was also godparent to William Henry's first son born in 1812.

The Dawnay's main residence was Cowick Hall and later Wykeham Abbey near Scarborough. William became 6th Viscount Downe in 1832, resigned his church livings and moved to Beningbrough along with his wife. During the 1830s they made various improvements to the Hall and grounds including installing a gallery over the main hall and transforming two ground floor rooms into a sizeable Drawing Room, essential for entertaining guests. Following the Viscount's death in 1846 and his widow's two years later, the estates were inherited by their younger son, Payan, and daughter, Lydia.

Brother and sister are noted as living a quiet life together in the house devoting themselves to public-spirited activities and the welfare of their tenants. Between 1848 and 1855 the pair organised the rebuilding of several churches including those at Shipton, Newton and Overton as well as building and maintaining two schools. Involved in some of the work was Yorkshire railway architect G.T. Andrews.

Lydia died in 1890 and her brother a year later and

the next in line at Beningbrough was the pair's nephew, Lieutenant-Colonel Lewis Payn Downay. Having resigned his commission in the Coldstream Guards, he was elected to Parliament, representing Thirsk until 1892. Thereafter, he actively campaigned for the Tory party. He moved to Beningbrough with his wife and four children during August 1892, this being the first time in more than a century that the house was occupied as family home.

Former Beningbrough administrator Michael Beaufoy with marble bust of Pope Clement XIV. [YP]

Family members involved themselves in a number of activities at Beningbrough including skating on the pond in winter, cricket in the summer, putting on theatrical performances in the Great Hall and crazily 'tobogganing' down the Main Staircase on tea trays.

Over the next 20 years the house and its surroundings were improved, including adding the Conservatory and New Service Wing; the forecourt remodelled; the installation of electricity; and all the farm buildings modernised.

The eldest son Major Guy Dawnay, inherited Beningbrough on the death of his father in 1910. He was 32 and by this time had left the army to become a merchant banker. Recalled by the Army in 1914, two years later he took the decision to put the estate up for sale. Amongst the probable reasons for his decision were to pay the final amounts of his father's death duty; his wife did not care for Beningbrough; and his work dictated he had to be in the London area.

Conducted by Messrs Knight, Frank & Rutley in York, the Beningbrough sale took place on November 14, 1916 and there was a very large company present. The auctioneer intimated that General Dawnay was prepared to take a low figure for the estate as a whole rather than sell some portions and have the remainder left on his hands.

Bidding started at £135,000, and W.A. Towler, of Littleport, Cambridgeshire, became the purchaser at £137,000. It was announced that Mr Towler intended to sell in lots as originally proposed, and the property was subsequently offered, several farms selling well.

Major Guy Dawnay © *National Trust*

Lewis Dawnay and family © *National Trust*

Lady Chesterfield, daughter of wealthy ship owner, Charles Wilson of Hull eventually bought the Hall, Home Farm and Park comprising approx. 375 acres for £15,000. Her husband, Edwyn, 10th Earl of Chesterfield, was more than twice her age and he had held posts in the Royal household. They moved to Beningbrough from Holme Lacy in Hertfordshire in July 1917.

Transforming the Hall and adapting it to their personal, lavish taste with pictures, furnishings and carvings, it became a great period of restoration for the house.

Lord Chesterfield spent much of his time in London leaving his wife in the north and they had no children. One of Lady Chesterfield's main interests at Beningbrough came from establishing a stud farm in the early 1920s. One of her successes was a black colt named 'Sun Castle' which she led in at Doncaster after winning the 1941 St Leger.

Beningbrough Hall was requisitioned by the RAF during WWII becoming host to airmen stationed at the Linton-on-Ouse base. During this time many of the house's contents were put in storage and Lady Chesterfield retreated to Home Farm. She did not return to the Hall until 1947 and died there in November 1957.

Fortunately, the house and estate were accepted by the government in lieu of death duties amounting to £29,250 and taken over by the National Trust. A four day sale of most of the Hall's contents took place only months after Lady Chesterfield's death.

The National Trust only had limited funds to buy

Enid, Countess of Chesterfield, by Elis Roberts, 1900.
© *National Trust*

RAF personnel outside Beningbrough Hall
© *National Trust*

items because it was felt they mainly belonged to the Chesterfields and so did not have any special long association with the house. Items acquired by the Trust included a few family portraits, the great state bed from Holme Lacy, marquetry pier-tables and glasses in the Drawing Room. The cost of the items purchased amounted to £10,000 which came from the National Land Fund.

Beningbrough Hall first opened to the public, with a curator installed, in 1961 but struggled financially until the mid-1970s when a decision was taken to transform the house into a major tourist attraction.

Lady Chesterfield with Sun Castle © *National Trust*

Above: Cleaners Ruby Coates (left) and Mrs Rachel Borrill at Beningbrough, March 1985. [YP]

Archaeological dig October 1991 to establish 'mystery missing wing' seen on 1751 painting. [YP]

Below: Beningbrough Hall's head gardener Michael Walker October, 1986. [YP]

Michael Beaufoy with Beningbrough Coat of Arms, June 1986. [YP]

View in Beningbrough's Gardens. © *National Trust*

The roof lead-work was renewed, the top floor strengthened and dry rot eradicated. Once all structural priorities were concluded an extensive scheme of redecorating the interior followed.

One of the first priorities was to fill the house with some worthwhile objects and to this end the National Portrait Gallery made a timely entry providing a sizeable loan of late 17th and early 18th century portraits. In later years the collections were augmented by furniture donated to the National Trust by Lady Megaw and a collection of ornamental porcelain given by Miss Dorothy Bushell. In more recent years there have been loans from the Ashmolean and Victoria & Albert Museums.

In 2006 the National Trust worked in harmony with the National Portrait Gallery and with the Heritage Lottery Fund to refurbish, redisplay and enhance access to Beningbrough Hall.

On the first and second floors *Making Faces* presents several user-friendly interpretation/interactive galleries for the National Portrait Gallery's collection. For instance in *Getting the Picture*, high

Parent and children in the interactive galleries.
© *National Trust*

and low-tech activities include *Virtual Portrait*, a *Portrait Sitting* and *Finishing Off*. These let a visitor commission an 18th century-style portrait from a virtual artist; make their own living portrait; and discover the tricks that artists employed to achieve results.

Part of the ongoing restoration of Beningbrough has been the nurturing of the gardens and parkland where sights, sounds and tastes are cultivated. Produce from the Walled Garden is even used in the in the Restaurant. The new Community Orchard and the beautiful Pear Arch in the gardens are particular treats.

Bramham Park

After a disastrous fire in 1828 Bramham Park house lay derelict for the remainder of the19th century. Rebuilt prior to WWI, when many other country houses and estates were being demolished and broken up, Bramham is now a thriving tourist attraction. The grounds play host to one of the country's foremost rock music events, as well as providing the setting for the annual Bramham International Horse Trials

The original house was built between 1698-1710 in a loosely Baroque style of architecture by Robert Benson, 1st Baron Bingley (c.1676-1731). Interestingly, Chatsworth House, Britain's first Baroque house was built between 1687-1707 and is contemporary with Bramham.

Benson had taken inspiration for Bramham from his Grand Tour, especially the Italian architecture and French garden design, though the building's architect remains unknown. Names suggested include James Gibbs, Thomas Archer, William Talman and James Paine. Paine later enhanced the stables with a clock

Current owner of Bramham Park, Nick Lane Fox poses with a portrait of Robert Benson (1st Lord Bingley) 1675–1731, the builder of the house. [YP]

View of Bramham Park c. 1825 by Henry Bryan Ziegler (1798–1874)

Bramham Park gates c. 1825 by Henry Bryan Ziegler (1798-1874)

tower, classical portico and flanking pavilions.

It is strongly speculated that Benson himself worked hand in hand with a local draughtsman to complete the design which is in a restrained French Baroque style. Yet, Bramham has two flanking wings – housing the kitchen and the chapel – more in the Palladian style.

Additionally, Benson is thought to have submitted

Harriet Benson (1705-1771)

ideas for the Gardens, Park and Woodlands. Contemporaries are on record as admiring his architectural knowledge and taste. He was consulted by the Duke of Chandos over Canons and by the Wentworth family at Wentworth Castle, near Barnsley.

Colen Campbell included the east elevation and plan of Bramham in his 1717 2nd Volume of *Vitruvius Britannicus*.

Niklaus Pevsner in *Yorkshire: The West Riding (1959)* said 'Bramham Park is a grand unusual house, but its gardens are grander and even more unusual. The house at Bramham was designed as a part of the whole landscape scheme: simply an element within it. This and the fact that it was designed only as a summer holiday residence, perhaps explain its relatively modest size'.

Robert Benson was elected Lord Mayor of York for 1707; MP for Thetford, Norfolk 1702-1705; MP for York, 1705-1713. Described as a moderate Tory, he was Chancellor of the Exchequer and ennobled as Lord Bingley in 1713 and became British Ambassador to Spain though never got there. As a director of the South Seas Company, an angry mob reputedly stoned his carriage in Cavendish Square after the South Sea Bubble burst. Nonetheless, he found favour with Queen Anne who visited

George Fox Lane (2nd Lord Bingley) 1697-1773

Bramham at least once and a portrait of her by Kneller still survives in the Hall.

On dying in 1731, Benson was buried in Westminster Abbey and the barony became extinct. He married Elizabeth the daughter of Hon. Heneage Finch and they had a son (who predeceased Robert) and two daughters Harriet and Mary (who was illegitimate). Reputedly, he also had an illegitimate son, the British soldier, dramatist and politician John Burgoyne, whose debts he cancelled in his will.

The remains of Benson's estate passed to Harriet (c.1705-1771) who had married George Fox (c. 1697-1773). In 1750, George took the additional name of Lane on succeeding to the estates of his maternal half-uncle, James Lane, 2nd Viscount Lanesborough. George was given the re-created title of Baron Bingley in 1762.

The Obelisk c. 1825 by Henry Bryan Ziegler (1798-1874)

James Fox Lane (1774-1821)

The Chapel c.1825 by Henry Bryan Ziegler (1798-1874)

During Harriet and George's tenure at Bramham, a number of additions were made to the Grounds. These included the Chapel built around 1760 to the designs of James Paine and originally built as a Palladian Temple. It was later used as an Orangery, a Summer House and consecrated as a Chapel around 1906. Standing in the Black Fen pleasure ground, the Ionic Temple or Rotunda was also designed by Paine. It was constructed in the form of a circular Ionic Temple on a 3-step podium with a colonnade of 16 un-fluted Ionic columns supporting an entablature.

George and Harriet's only son and heir, the Hon, Robert Fox Lane, MP for York, predeceased them in 1768. He had no children and his parents

George Lane Fox 'The Gambler' (1793-1848)

commissioned John Carr of York to build the Obelisk in Black Fen, in his memory.

The barony became extinct for a second time when George died in 1773; Harriet had died two years earlier. Bramham then passed to Robert Benson's illegitimate daughter Mary who married Sir John Goodricke of Ribston Hall. The couple were allegedly responsible for taking away a proportion of Bramham's household silver, Sheraton furniture, stone garden ornaments and cutting down 'a fine oak wood'.

On Mary's death in 1792, Bramham, now reduced in value, was inherited by James Fox (1756-1821). He became Fox-Lane from 1773 and was a nephew of George Fox Lane and Harriet. Elected MP for Horsham in 1804, he was a close friend of the Prince Regent who frequently visited Bramham to go fox-hunting. James also turned the family surname round to 'Lane Fox'.

Following James' death, a dark period began. The house and estates were inherited by his son George Lane-Fox (1793-1848), known by reputation as 'the Gambler'. Standing 6ft 5in in his stockings and boasting good looks and a magnificent physique, George was a hard-drinking, gambling man and deeply in debt at the time of his father's death. He had married Georgiana Buckley in 1814 but this was an unsuccessful partnership and they eventually separated. Growing to a massive 19 stone, George was away in Dorset, at the funeral of his uncle Lord Rivers, when the house at Bramham was reduced to ruins by fire early on Tuesday morning July 29, 1828. Thankfully, there were no casualties.

Reporting on the incident, the *London Courier and Evening Gazette* on Friday August 1, 1828 attempted to relay the sense of anxiety and horror that must have been felt at the time: 'The fire commenced about one o'clock. All exertions to save the mansion were unavailing, and that all the inmates escaped with their lives may be considered a matter of

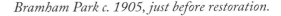

Bramham Park c. 1905, just before restoration.

THE OLD HALL BRAMHAM PARK.

Bramham Park c. 1905, just before restoration; note the large tree which has grown since the time of the fire.

George Lane Fox 'The Squire' (1810-1896)

surprise. Let those accustomed to the busy life of London imagine themselves in the centre of a park, no neighbour nearer than some half mile or more – all nature hushed – and at or near the solemn hour of midnight – thus situated to be awakened from their first sleep. Let them for a moment imagine such a situation – present to their minds such a picture, and it may fearlessly be said nothing can or could be more appalling. This picture is not a fiction – such was the fact, and to hear the tales (oft told no doubt) of the inmates, would indeed harrow up the soul even of the most frigid. The calamity was of that nature, the astonishment of all was so great, that soon after the morning's dawn hundreds were to be seen bending their course towards the spot to see a sight so rare, and such a one as thousands had never seen before, and it may be hoped will never see again'.

The cause of the ferocious fire was allegedly due to a footman, carousing in the servants' hall in the butler's absence, and he drunkenly upset an oil lamp. Many of Robert Benson's treasures were lost including tapestries and a massive collection of solid silver plate. Two of George's younger daughters and their nurse, who had been asleep upstairs, narrowly cheated death by scurrying across the roofs to safety.

A billiard table recently delivered to the hall created much confusion during the calamity. Trying to wrestle it outside, the table became stuck in the main doorway thwarting the rescue of many valuable objects.

Unable to afford rebuilding the property, George and his family spent time at the nearby Bowcliffe Hall and Hope Hall; Bramham lay derelict for the next 80 years. George represented Beverley and Pontefract successively in Parliament, and was again member for Beverley from 1837 to 1841. He was a major in the Yorkshire Yeoman Cavalry, and Deputy

James Lane Fox 'The Soldier' (1841–1906)

Lieutenant for the North Riding.

On George's death at the age of 55, his eldest son, also called George (1810–1896), succeeded. Known as the Squire, he had a difficult time trying to pay off his father's gambling debts totalling some £150,000, but they were eventually cleared.

The Squire's elder son, another George, had a

George Lane Fox 'The Politician' (1870–1947). [YP]

vocation for the priesthood, so father and son agreed that he would not succeed to the estate. The youngest son James (b.1841) took over in 1896. Educated at Eton, he subsequently joined the Grenadier Guards, retiring in 1867 with the rank of Captain. The Prince of Wales, the later King Edward VII, was honorary colonel of the Grenadier Guards and formed a life-long friendship with James.

Unfortunately, James did not enjoy good health after a serious fall from a horse whilst out hunting and died in 1906.

'He wor a reight gentleman, tek' him any roads ye' like' embodied the opinion of every man in Bramham and every tenant of the Bramham estates,' the *Leeds Mercury* reported on Tuesday February 27, 1906.

James was succeeded by his son George Lane Fox (1870–1947) who, in 1903, had married Agnes, the daughter of 2nd Viscount Halifax. This was around the time Government legislation was implemented to compulsory purchase land in Ireland, including the Lane Fox's Irish Leitrim estates covering some 12,000 acres. With this compensation and a dowry, plus finance from other sales, the couple were able to fulfil a promise George had made to his grandfather – that he would rebuild the derelict house at Bramham.

Bramham Park Gothic Temple 18 August 1958. [YP]

Architect Detmar Blow (1867–1939) was employed to re-create the original house as painstakingly as possible. The bay window on the West Front, which had been added to the original design, was removed and replaced with steps modelled on Fontainbleau.

The family reoccupied the building just over 80 years after the devastating fire. On the outbreak of WWI, George Lane Fox served with the Yorkshire Hussars and was wounded. During the hostilities the house was a convalescent home for wounded officers; the family occupying a smaller area.

George Lane Fox had been elected to Parliament in 1906 and held several government posts including Secretary of State for Mines in 1923. Ten years later, he was made Lord Bingley (third creation).

During WWII, Bramham was initially home to evacuee children and there was a prisoner of war camp in the woods and amongst the prisoners were Cossacks. A convalescent home was also established for a period in the house.

George Lane Fox had four daughters and on his death the title became extinct once more. His eldest daughter, Marcia (1904-1980), married Joe Ward-Jackson (an officer in the Household Cavalry) in 1929 and eight years later, he adopted her maiden name, Lane Fox.

During the couple's tenure of the rebuilt house, repairs were undertaken on the temples in the grounds and ornamental stonework. They also replaced old trees particularly after the Great Gale of 1962, when 400 mature beech trees were uprooted.

Bramham Park interior, The Hall

Many country estates in the post-war years had to establish a modern business plan to survive. Marcia and Joe's son, George Lane Fox, was instrumental in achieving this for Bramham. After 20 years in the Household Cavalry, he developed the in-hand farming business and the forestry, starting the Bramham International Horse Trials in 1974.

Aerial view of Bramham Park 18 June 1935. [YP]

Bramham Park interior

Additionally, the house and grounds became used for filming and other events on a regular basis.

From 1997, George's eldest son Nick, along with his wife Rachel and their family of five children, moved into the house and he took over the management of the estate from his father. Since then, Nick has further developed and diversified the estate's business. Most notably, the Leeds Rock Festival which moved to Bramham in 2003. This has further

The Hon. Mrs. M. A. M. Lane Fox and Colonel Francis G. Lane Fox. [YP]

enhanced the estate and allowed the restoration of the southern parkland, ploughed out during WWII.

Prominent interior rooms presently to be seen at Bramham include the Hall which is a perfect cube, 10m square. For 80 years after the fire, a temporary roof protected the area. The effects of weathering can be seen in the walls. The Gallery was formerly three smaller rooms before the fire and afterwards was

used for dancing. The North Room is where Queen Anne is thought to have slept when she visited Bramham. The Library accommodates all the books that remained after the fire from Robert Benson's original collection. Many of them are fire damaged.

Nick Lane Fox and wife, Rachel, continue to develop Bramham, the 10th generation of the creator's family, working very hard to preserve it for the next 300 years.

Centre, George Lane Fox 1931-2012, and son Nick Lane Fox. [YP]

Nick Lane Fox walks by some of the structures being built at Bramham Park for Leeds Festival, 2010. [YP]

Brodsworth Hall

My last visit to Brodsworth Hall, near Doncaster, was one Sunday afternoon in the mid 1980s. I was taking tea with the surviving inhabitant of the great Victorian mansion, octogenarian Sylvia Grant-Dalton. Looking forward to a veritable feast of freshly cut sandwiches, chicken legs, trifles, sticky buns and cream cakes not to mention a sip of wine, I was very disappointed when she casually requested her cook George Matson to prepare asparagus soup.

She was extremely worried about the Hall's fate on her death, which she bleakly anticipated was not far away. The house was crippled with subsidence - one part of the building surviving in its former astonishing splendour whilst much of the rest was derelict.

She said her only daughter Pamela was not interested in prolonging the life of the Hall and estate and even if she were, death duties were liable to seriously thwart any plans of continuity.

A number of stately homes in the immediate vicinity such as Sprotbrough Hall and Crookhill Hall had been demolished whilst others had been insensitively converted for other uses. In fact, very few in

The 18th century house with Brodsworth church in the background [Author's collection]

Yorkshire still existed as private homes with extensive estates.

Sylvia Grant Dalton perhaps surprised me with her remarkable enthusiasm for Brodsworth Hall and its estates mainly because she was not a direct descendant of the Thellusson family who built the house yet she had lived there for over 50 years.

The 18th century house [Author's collection]

The evolution towards the present house perhaps began in the early 18th century. A modest manor house at Brodsworth and its estate, which can be traced back the 11th century, was bought by George Hay, Viscount Dupplin, eldest son and heir to Thomas, seventh Earl of Kinnoull. Eventually becoming the eighth Earl of Kinnoull in 1719, he probably rebuilt or improved the property, besides laying out pleasure gardens and woodland walks and planting trees across the estate.

He lost his fortune in the South Sea Bubble speculation in 1720 and did not spend much time with his wife and ten children at Brodsworth, becoming British ambassador to the Sublime Porte in Constantinople, between 1729-1736.

The Eighth Earl, George Hay died in 1758 and his eldest son Thomas succeeded him, becoming ninth Earl of Kinnoull. But, George's second son, Robert Hay Drummond, took up residence at Brodsworth, once he had become Archbishop of York in 1761.

Under his tenure, during the 1770s, the house underwent major rebuilding and photographs taken during the mid-19th century reveal a hipped roof and bays on the south and east facades. The interior included seven Bedchambers, two Drawing Rooms, two Dining Rooms, a Hall, Library and Study.

The Archbishop died in 1777 and in time the Kinnoull title and lands passed, once elder brother Thomas had died in 1787, to the former's son, Robert Auriol. He sold the Brodsworth house and estate to wealthy merchant and banker, Peter Thellusson, in 1791.

He had built up his fortune providing shipping and cargo credit and insurance. He was also involved with the West Indian sugar trade. Before acquiring the Brodsworth estate he built a Palladian villa at Plaistow near Bromley in Kent. Dying in 1797, he chose to be buried at Brodsworth.

Peter Thellusson's will caused an immediate and lengthy controversy and was not settled until a final legal judgement came in 1858. During the intervening period his youngest son, Charles (1770-1815) spent some time at Brodsworth. His son also called Charles (1797-1856) had a passion for horse racing and his horse 'Rataplan' won the Doncaster Gold Cup in 1855.

The latter Charles had a son, Charles Sabine Augustus Thellusson (b.1822), who became one of two beneficiaries of the protracted Peter Thelusson will settlement. Charles Sabine spent a few years as a Captain in the 12th Royal Lancers before marrying wealthy Georgiana Theobald in 1850. The couple

Water colour drawing of the new Brodsworth Hall ©Historic England Archive

rented Brighton's Marlbrough House for ten years and Charles Sabine was a major figure in British yachting. He commissioned innovative and successful sailing yachts and amongst these was the fastest and largest of their day, *The Aline*. The yacht was commissioned in 1860 and eventually won the Queen's Cup. Charles Sabine was Commodore of the Isle of Wight's Royal Victoria Yacht Club

On 29 March 1860 the *Doncaster Gazette* reported that Charles Sabine Augustus Thellusson, owner of the Brodsworth estate, was about to erect a new property. This was on a site a short distance away from the existing Georgian house which stood near to the village church. To have the entire house built and furnished, to landscape and plant the gardens, and provide estate cottages cost around £50,000.

The new house's building work was undertaken by London contractors Longmire & Burge under the direction of a little-known London architect, Philip Wilkinson who is otherwise credited with designing housing in London.

During the rebuilding period one man was seriously injured and another killed. The fatality occurred when a portico fell on 37 year-old John Hall the foreman of the stonemasons whilst he was directing the removal of stone supports.

A month later, on May 2 1863, the *Doncaster Gazette*, seemingly oblivious to the construction of the Hall's cost in human terms, reported: 'The damage sustained by the fall of the portico at Brodsworth Hall, the seat of Charles S. Thellusson, Esq will be little short of £800'.

The house was built and furnished in just 18 months between 1861 and 1863. Wilkinson's well-proportioned Italianate house re-used materials from the old house and stone quarried on the estate, combined with luxurious materials, such as scagliola and marble and hand-painted surfaces. The Bond Street firm of Lapworths was brought in to furnish the house.

A feature of the frontage was the columned porte-cochère enabling visitors to alight from carriages under cover from adverse weather conditions. All the principal rooms stretched behind the entrance in a large block with a servants' wing adjoining at right angles.

The house was built using white magnesian limestone from the estate and the entire design reflects a restrained Italianate style with tasteful detailing including urns on the balustrade and slight variations in the window surrounds.

The ground floor rooms include Entrance Hall and Inner Hall; Morning Room; Dining Room; South Hall; Billiard Room; Drawing Room; West Hall; and Library. The entire area is also noteworthy for the large group of 19th century sculpture which was an important mark of cultural and social prestige amongst country house owners. Brodsworth's interior sculptures were acquired at the 1865 Dublin International Exhibition. Nearly all the works were by supplied by Chevalier Casentini once erroneously thought to be the designer of the entire house.

Amongst the upstairs features are: the Bedroom Corridor; Family Bedrooms; the Principal Guest

Charles Thellusson and his wife Mary cut the first sod at Brodsworth colliery [Author's collection]

Room; Nurseries; Service Stairs; and Servants' Wing.

Work in the grounds, extending over 15 acres, continued for several more years under the supervision of the first head gardener (Samuel Taylor), head woodman and a number of specialist contractors. The gardens featured statuary - again supplied by sculptor Casentini - and the woodland was renovated. Further contracts were awarded to Longmire and Burge in the 1860s and 1870s for approach roads and dwellings for estate staff.

On moving his wife and their six children north to Brodsworth, Charles Sabine soon involved himself in local matters, becoming high sheriff for the West

Riding in 1865. He was a keen sportsman, employing approximately 10 gamekeepers to ensure excellent pheasant and partridge shoots over the estate.

After Charles Sabine's death in March 1885 the Brodsworth Hall estate was occupied in succession by his sons Peter, Charles and Augustus. In 1905, Charles leased land to the newly formed Brodsworth Colliery company, bringing income from rent and royalties on the coal mined until nationalisation in 1947. This additional finance was welcomed as income from the estate had been falling drastically since the end of the 19th century. It helped with major repairs to the house and estate buildings. Several rooms were decorated, the kitchen was updated and electricity was installed.

Charles was also able to live comfortably as the Brodsworth squire, entertaining, indulging in many yachting trips and fishing off Norway and Scotland.

Hall Gardens [Author's collection]

Brodsworth Hall and estate was depleted of staff during the 1914-18 conflict and staff numbers did not recover afterwards.

Charles Sabine's youngest son, Augustus, inherited the Brodsworth estate on his brother's death in 1919 when he was 56.

Augustus only lived at Brodsworth during the shooting season and the house wasn't kept like it had been in its Victorian and Edwardian heyday. On Augustus's death in 1931, the Brodsworth Hall estate passed to his nephew Charles Grant-Dalton (born 1884). Earlier, in 1916, Charles had married Sylvia West (born 1899), and they had one daughter, Pamela.

The small family moved from the Hampshire coast near Lymington to live at Brodsworth. But death duties forced the family to sell paintings from the house as well as a portion of the Marr estate situated nearby. Brodsworth's shooting rights were leased and the Kitchen Gardens let after 1941.

During the early part of WWII, the Hall was requisitioned for military use, becoming the headquarters first for General Arthur Percival of the 44th (Home Counties) Infantry and then for a series of army units. Sylvia and her daughter Pamela volunteered at the Warde Aldam hospital at Frickley during the hostilities.

In the post-war years, even fewer people were employed at Brodsworth and when Charles died in 1952, the estate was left in trust for his daughter, Pamela.

Sylvia subsequently married, in 1959, Eustace Grant-Dalton (born 1877), one of Charles' cousins, and he died in 1970. Thereafter, Sylvia, ever popular amongst the estate tenants and their families, continued to live at Brodsworth until her own death in 1988.

Sylvia's daughter, now Pamela Williams, donated the house and gardens to English Heritage, retaining ownership of the estate. The house's contents were

Brodsworth Hall January, 1989. [YP]

Sylvia Grant-Dalton. [YP]

Ronald and Pamela Williams. [YP]

The Drawing Room. [YP]

acquired for £3.36m by the National Heritage Memorial Fund and subsequently transferred to English Heritage. Brodsworth Hall's contents and interior were praised loudly as a perfectly preserved Victorian 'time capsule'. And, 'Preserved as found' was to be the theme on opening to the public in 1995.

Before this occurred the house underwent extensive

Entrance hall and staircase. ©Historic England Archive

repairs. Subsidence due to the house's close proximity to Brodsworth Main colliery had caused a number of major problems along with water seeping in through the leaking roof and down-pipes. The soft limestone exterior was badly affected by pollution and erosion. Insect infestation and sunlight flooding through the huge Victorian plate glass windows had also brought their own inherent problems.

On February 13, 1991 the *Yorkshire Post* reported that soaring above the scaffolding-girdled Brodsworth Hall, a 70-tonne mobile crane was swinging parts of a temporary roof into place to protect the Listed Grade One Victorian building's historic interior while the original slate roof was restored. It was many years since any major repairs were carried out to the roof and the work was the first phase of a £4m structural repair and conservation programme.

On July 5, 1995 Princess Margaret performed an opening ceremony at the Hall. She was met by local dignitaries, including Ronald Williams a former Commissioner of Police in Gibraltar and husband of the late Pamela who had died in 1994.

Greeting Princess Margaret, English Heritage chairman Jocelyn Stevens said: 'Five years ago we were entrusted with a marvellous Victorian house and its contents. Visitors from near and far will now be able to see how different generations lived at Brodsworth and admire the glories of the house and gardens'.

Just over twenty years on from Brodsworth Hall's grand opening, the house and gardens have welcomed many thousands of visitors. English Heritage has now had to undertake further work to the fabric of the building.

Brodsworth Hall restoration, February 1991. [YP]

Work on the roof taking place in January, 1992. [YP]

Of the £80 million investment from government into English Heritage since 2105 to work towards becoming a self-funding charity, £52 million was earmarked for addressing the most urgent conservation needs. Brodsworth has been one of the first properties to benefit from a large conservation project.

Highly skilled conservation work has been carried out to repair the historic revolving window shutters, replacing the heating system and repair the leaking skylights; its interiors remain conserved as they were found after Sylvia Grant-Dalton's death. The work has been undertaken in 2017.

In contrast to the 1990s, the public has been able to witness this as it progresses, and find out both about the causes of damage to the Hall - from subsidence and damp to insect pests and even Sylvia Grant-Dalton's pet dogs - and how the building is being cared for

So on a final note, I do hope Sylvia Grant-Dalton is looking down on the Hall and is delighted at what has happened since her death - and dining on something a little more exciting than asparagus soup.

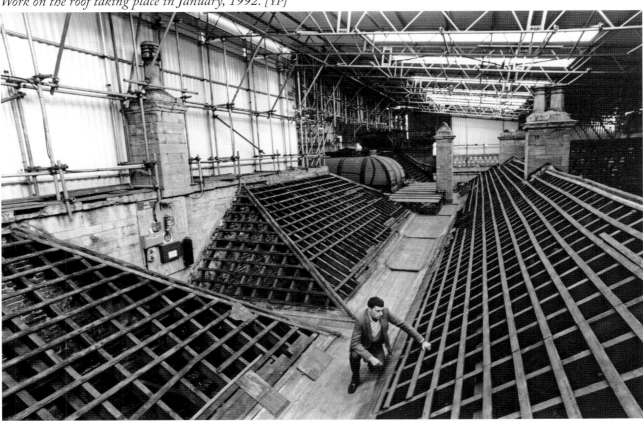

Burton Agnes

Few Yorkshire estates can claim to have never changed hands for centuries but Burton Agnes can. Ever since the Norman manor house was built there by Roger de Stuteville in 1173, the estate, situated midway between Driffield and Bridlington, has never changed hands by sale – though it has occasionally slid from family to family when the male line has ended.

One of Stuteville's daughters, named Agnes, may have been responsible for the name Burton Agnes, which was first recorded in a deed from c. 1175.

The Manor House still stands today, encased in uninspiring brick, an alteration dating from the 17th century, when it was used as a Laundry, whilst a Lower Chamber survives in all its gloomy Norman splendour. An upper room is thought to have been the Great Hall, developed in the mid-fifteenth century. Of course the Manor House would have been much larger than surviving fragments suggest. Only 20 Norman manor houses of this style and age remain in Britain; the one at Burton Agnes is

Manor House, The Great Hall

presently under the guardianship of English Heritage.

Surrounded by woodland, the present red brick Burton Agnes Hall, with stone plinth, quoins, mullions and ornaments, was built during the Elizabethan period – marked by stability, prosperity and growing confidence. It was also a time when landowners, grown rich on the flourishing agriculture, built sumptuous houses to show off their wealth and power.

Sir Henry Griffith, born 1558, was behind the new

Manor House, Lower chamber

Burton Agnes Hall scheme. His earlier ancestors lived for a period in de Struteville's twelfth century manor house, having re-roofed it and made it habitable.

Sir Henry Griffith depicted in a carving

Descending from a Welsh family, who had emigrated to Staffordshire in the thirteenth century, Sir Henry Griffith was appointed to the Council of the North, based in York, in 1599. Although he had already started building work on a new home in the Midlands, this was superseded by a Hall strategically sited at Burton Agnes and probably erected between 1598-1610.

The design work is attributed to Robert Smithson, operating at a time when the profession of architect was in its most embryonic stage of development and when houses were designed by surveyors and master masons. Smithson was trained as a stonemason, and by the 1560s was travelling England leading his own team of masons. His style is eclectic with Renaissance, Flemish, English Gothic traces to be found in his buildings.

Master Mason to Queen Elizabeth, Smithson was a builder much sought after and whose style defined the stately manors of the age. He was stonemason for the house at Longleat and later designed Hardwick Hall and Wollaton Hall.

Burton Agnes Hall, with its adherence to the principles of Tudor Renaissance architecture (Commoditie, Firmness and Delight), is the only Smithson house where the plan still exists, in the RIBA collection.

Noted architectural historian Mark Girouard in his definitive book on the Smithson family of architects, called grand and ornate Burton Agnes, set in idyllic grounds a 'splendid and glittering composition'. Simon Jenkins, author of *England's Thousand Best Houses*, added Burton Agnes Hall was 'the perfect English house' and one of the twenty best English

Burton Agnes by William Marlow 1740-1813

houses alongside Windsor Castle, Buckingham Palace and Chatsworth House.

The eastern skyline of the Hall is described as romantically irregular and shows how the front was built higher than the rear in order to accommodate the Long Gallery which spans the length of the house on the third floor. The Entrance faces south, its symmetry retained by the device of putting the Entrance Door at the side of the projecting bays. Above the entrance is the date 1601 with the initials of Sir Henry Griffith and his wife.

The Entrance Bay

Interior of Great Hall, drawing by Charles Richardson

The Great Hall

The Chinese Room

The King's State Bedroom

The Ground Floor includes the Screens Passage, the Great Hall, the Inner Hall, the Red Drawing Room, the Chinese Room, the Garden Gallery, the dining Room, and the Staircase

In the Great Hall, the Elizabethan carving, plasterwork and panelling is considered to be matchless. The chimney piece in the Drawing Room features a further outstanding example of Elizabethan carving. The main panel is a gruesome 'Dance of Death'.

Amongst the first floor rooms are the White Drawing Room, the King's State Bedroom, the Justices' Room, the Queen's State Bedroom, and the Music Gallery.

Originally known as the Great Chamber, the White Drawing Room was formerly used to entertain important visitors, who would dine and be entertained by musicians, jugglers and plays in the area. Interestingly, in the King's State Bedroom the doors have a unique locking device: the door could be opened and locked via a system of cords and pulleys without the occupant getting out of bed. The magnificent 17th century bed, still hung with some of the original blue damask, is Italian and is known as either an 'Angel' or 'Flying Tester' bed. In the Queen's State Bedroom an amazing and complex feature is the original moulded Jacobean plasterwork on the ceiling. The chimney piece is flanked by a pair of Corinthian columns and its over mantel is divided into three panels by further columns. The magnificent bed was made in 1729 for Sewerby House, near Bridlington and was brought to Burton Agnes in 1934.

On the second floor is the Long Gallery, the Library, and the Reading Room. The Long Gallery was initially used for exercise, particularly by ladies when the weather was unsuitable for walking outside.

Old view of the Long Gallery

The Queen's State Bedroom

Modern view of the Long Gallery

The three Griffith sisters; Katherine is on the right

Carefully watching the new Burton Agnes house being built was Katherine (Anne) Griffith, the youngest of Sir Henry Griffith's three daughters. Apparently, she could talk and think of nothing else, firmly believing it would be the most beautiful house ever built. Around the time of completion, she ventured out alone one afternoon to visit the St Quintins at Harpham about a mile away accompanied by her dog.

At dusk she set off for home and when near St. John's Well was clubbed and robbed by cut-throats and vagabonds. Eventually brought home to Burton Agnes badly hurt, Katherine was sometimes delirious, sometimes sensible, telling her sisters she would never rest unless part of her could remain in 'our beautiful home as long as it shall last'. She made them make a gruesome promise: when she was dead her head should be severed and preserved in the Hall forever. To pacify her, both sisters, although

horrified, agreed but on her death, she was interred in the churchyard.

Because the macabre promise was broken, it is alleged, she haunted the new house, scaring the life out of everybody. These weird events encouraged her two sisters to open the grave and bring her skull into the house. As long as the skull remained undisturbed, there were seemingly no ghostly goings on in the Hall.

On one occasion the skull was thrown away, another time it was buried in the garden but when that happened a ghost allegedly walked with tremendous noise and upheaval. Sightings of a strange lady in the Hall and sometimes the smell of lavender or violets in the rooms when no one has been in have continued to be an eerie feature of the house in the ensuing years.

Katherine's sister, Frances Griffith, married Sir Mathew Boynton 1st Bt, and their grandson

William Boynton was the first member of the Boynton family to reside at Burton Agnes. His son Sir Griffith Boynton 3rd Baronet made many alterations to the house, particularly to the White Drawing Room.

Passing down several generations of Boyntons and Baronets, which extended through the Queen Anne, Georgian, Regency and Victorian periods, the Burton Agnes estate was home to several colourful characters. Sir Francis Boynton (1777-1832) 8th Bt. bred famous gamecocks to fight in the cockpit, the site still existing in the Park field to the east of Burton Agnes Hall. Sir Henry Somerville Boynton 11th Bt (1844-1899) was a great naturalist and kept aviaries at the Hall and also had a large collection of stuffed birds.

Marcus Wickham-Boynton

Cyceley Boynton (1877-1947)

Sir Henry's daughter Cyceley Boynton (1877-1947) inherited the Burton Agnes estate. Her husband Thomas Lamplugh Wickham (1869-1942) assumed the name and arms of Boynton. Their eldest son, Major Henry Faifax Wickham-Boynton (b. 1900), was killed on active service in 1942 and so the estate passed to his brother Marcus Wickham-Boynton (b. 1904).

Marcus was born and raised at Burton Agnes. After an education at Eton, he later developed an interest in both agriculture and breeding race horses. Working as the land agent for the Highclere Castle Estate in Berkshire he had some dealings with the London-based Adams' Gallery which dealt in French Impressionist and other works. He began collecting works of art in a small way from around 1937.

For a time Wickham-Boynton worked at breeding stables near Paris and was quite aware of the buoyancy of modern art movements in the city. Because there was a risk of the Adams' Gallery pictures being damaged during WWII in London, the owners asked Wickham-Boynton if some of them could be stored at his house on the Highclere estate.

Living for several years amongst many stunning art works, including those by Matisse, Duffy, Modigliani and Picasso, displayed in his bedroom and sitting room, this nurtured further a passion for art as well as a deep desire to collect.

He added more pictures to his growing collection at a period when works by French artists were affordable and not fetching the astronomical prices

Flowers by Duncan Grant

Woman shelling peas, Camille Pissarro

Painting by Augustus John

Head of a Tahitian woman, Paul Gauguin

of today. Two art collector friends who helped or advised him were Lord Ivor Spencer Churchill and the Right Hon. Harcourt 'Crinks' Johnstone. His appreciation of French Impressionists owed much to the influence of Samuel Courtauld. The directors of the Adams' Gallery gave him much valuable advice and help in the choice of individual paintings.

On the death of his brother and father in 1942 Marcus was suddenly left to take over at Burton Agnes and was not pleased. Reluctantly, he moved back home to live with his ageing, formidable mother, Cycely (1877-1947), the couple never enjoying a good relationship.

He took on the management of the house and estate in a troubled time; there were mortgages on some of the land and the house was not in a good state of repair. Over his lifetime at Burton Agnes he reversed both situations and built up the estate to the fabulous place it is today.

Marcus Wickham-Boynton and Simon Cunliffe-Lister

Painting by Henri Matisse

Described by close friends and employees as a fair yet demanding and well organised man, Wickham-Boynton was very successful as an arable farmer and as a breeder of racehorses, establishing a stud at Burton Agnes. All this went some way to finance renovations in the house particularly the conversion of the Long Gallery on the third floor back to its original condition. This took place over a long period and in several stages starting in 1951. The room stretches the full width of the house, and is where many of the modern French paintings presently hang round the walls. The work was carried out under the supervision of a local architect, Francis Johnson, FRIBA.

This ambitious activity sharply contrasted with the decline of many country houses throughout the country in the post-War years . In fact cooks, butlers and a chauffeur could still be seen at Burton Agnes in Wickham-Boynton's lifetime.

Throughout his life, he continued to buy and sell paintings. Unfortunately this included the sale of number of Impressionist works and a small painting by Bonnard. Nonetheless, the Long Gallery remains a testament to his prowess as a shrewd, yet adventurous, pioneer art collector.

Initially, when he included the bright – some would say garish – French paintings at 17th century Burton Agnes, the reaction was one of shock and disgust. Perhaps today the equivalent would be exhibiting one of Damien Hirst's works – a cow in formaldehyde – in the house. Now, safely snuggling into the history of art, the French pictures fit in quite comfortably amongst the formal family portraits and classical landscapes.

The entire collection of Wickham-Boynton paintings is really quite broad, ranging from the work of French Realists Corot (1796-1875) and Courbet (1819-1877), through to the Impressionists Pissaro (1830-1913) and Renoir (1841-1919), then Post

Modern sculture displayed in the Long Gallery

Impressionists such as Derain (1880-1954), Gauguin (1848-1903) and Matisse (1869-1954).

There are paintings by early 20th century English artists and sculptors who absorbed the influence from across the channel and include Duncan Grant (1885-1978), Augustus John (1878-1961) and Jacob Epstein (1880-1959).

Wickham-Boynton never had children or married and in 1977 gave Burton Agnes Hall, 42 acres (17 hectacres) of surrounding gardens and grounds, over 600 acres (243 hectacres) of good agricultural land plus a cash endowment to the trustees of a registered charity. It was formed for the protection and upkeep of Burton Agnes Hall and its historic contents.

Marcus Wickham-Boynton died in 1989 and the registered charity ensures that the Hall remains well cared for and open to visitors for at least six months of the year. It also remains a lived in family home, occupied by descendents of the Boynton family, having passed through the female line via Mary Constance Boynton to Simon Cunliffe-Lister who was only 12 years old when his uncle, Marcus Whickham-Boynton, died.

'He was a typical Yorkshire man who was very adept in finding good deals for pictures to add to his collection,' quipped Simon who quite freely admits his uncle's collection is something to be very proud of.

Today Marcus Wickham-Boynton's enthusiasm for art continues to thrive at Burton-Agnes with 'an artist in residence' scheme. During the months when the Hall is open, diverse artists stay, usually in pairs, to spend time in the Summer House studio and around the Hall and Gardens. Art work is displayed in the Summer House and inside the Hall. The Courtyard Gallery also, separately, houses a year-round programme of local artists, who display and sell their work.

Simon Cunliffe-Lister outside Burton Agnes Hall. [YP]

Burton Constable

In 2016, Burton Constable Hall staged an informative exhibition to mark the 300th anniversary of the birth of England's greatest gardener Lancelot Brown or – as he is most widely known – 'Capability' Brown. This was quite fitting because in the late 18th century he made a remarkable contribution to the estate much of which is visible today.

'Capability' stuck because he would frequently inform titled and wealthy clients their land had great capability for improvement. Over his 67 years he transformed the face of the English countryside, designing about 250 impressive parks. His picturesque style can still be seen in Yorkshire, in particular at Burton Constable which is the best documented example of his work in the county.

Born as a yeoman farmer's fifth child, in Kirkharle, Northumberland, he left school aged 16 to work as an apprentice in the Kitchen Garden at Kirkharle Hall, staying there until 23.

His first landscape commission was a new lake in the park at Kiddington Hall. In 1740, he worked under William Kent, at Lord Cobham's Stowe Park, Bucks where a major parkland overhaul was in progress.

At 26, in 1742, he became Head Gardener at Stowe with an annual salary of £25 and during that time was allowed to take commissions from Cobham's extremely rich friends; his reputation flourishing. After Cobham's death in 1749, Brown set up his own business, work largely coming via recommendations. He also designed a few buildings.

Brown was sought after by landed families wanting something unique for their huge estates. In 1764 he was appointed as Surveyor to his Majesty's Gardens and Waters at Hampton Court, with a considerable annual salary of £2,000.

Fortunately for Brown, in the 1700s, it was fashionable to improve estates which made him very

Burton Constable from the East, Anglo–Dutch School. c.1685

William Constable (1721-1791)

busy. His work took years to complete and involved hundreds of men using only horses and simple hand tools. No-one had designed landscapes like his before as taste dictated more formal gardens but Brown changed all that. He was quite visionary. Landowners loved him but not everyone liked his style.

A speciality was making his landscapes look so natural, though they were meticulously planned and he was renowned for creating amazing views. Often he used a local landmark like a church or a castle as a focal point. They were practical as well as pretty as he created arable and pasture land by draining water into huge new lakes which became something of a Brown trademark.

He planted thousands of trees and frequently used ha-ha's – a sunken wall to restrict cattle movement without spoiling the view. He visited clients and staff by horse, despite suffering badly from asthma throughout his life taking days to travel from one place to another, in all weathers and in harsh, dangerous conditions.

Capability Brown was at East Yorkshire's Burton Constable Hall – the home of the Constable family – to landscape the park during the last years of his life.

The Constable family added their name to the manor at Burton following acquisition through marriage in the late 12th century. Significant building work took place in the late fifteenth century when a new brick manor house was built and in time this replaced Halsham as the family's main residence. During the 1560s much of this was demolished when the wealthy Sir John Constable (c.1526-1579), started rebuilding.

Construction work was continued after Sir John's death by his son, Sir Henry (c.1559-1608). Amongst the remains of the old manor house incorporated into the new property were the North Lodgings Wing and North Tower (known as St Stephens Tower surviving from the 12th century). Both areas were 'modernised' to include new stone mullioned windows and mock quoins to blend with the new structure. Sections added included a new range with a Great Hall, Parlour and Great Chamber as well as a South Wing incorporating a tower to match with the surviving North Tower.

By the end of the 16th century, further developments had occurred most notably the building to the west of a new range of lodging rooms with a Gallery.

A c.1685 view of the Hall, although not showing the rear gardens, provides an indication as to the formal layout and approach to the house. Glimpses may be seen of the Tudor fishponds at the rear.

William Constable (1721-1791) on inheriting the estate in 1747 was intent on extensively remodelling both the house and park in line with contemporary styles. Like many Gentlemen of the day, William Constable went on the Grand Tour picking up ideas and schemes. Work on demolishing and rebuilding the whole north western section of the house which had been started in the earlier part of the 18th century was not completed until the 1770s. In that area William Constable's replacement buildings included a Billiard Room and Grand Drawing Room with bedrooms above. He sacrificed the Elizabethan great bay on the East Front to allow the building of a pedimented central entrance in place of the outmoded doorway at the South End. The Elizabethan stables on the Hall's North Side were cleared and in their place built a grand new block further away to the south.

William Constable's remodelling of the house interior involved schemes for the Great Hall and the Dining Room. Rising to the full height of the building, the Great Hall dominated the Elizabethan house but, arguably, had been spoiled in previous years by the lowering of the ceiling and the upper windows being blanked off. Also an elaborate carved stone screen at the southern end had been demolished. Details below give some idea of the alterations carried out in certain rooms.

The Great Hall

William's alterations in the Great Hall were carried out to the plans of Timothy Lightoler (1727-1769). Other designs were commissioned by John Carr (1723-1807); and 'Capability' Brown (1716-1783) but rejected. A huge main door to the house was intended to blend with the existing Elizabethan windows. James Henderson (fl. 1755-1787) of York was responsible for the decorative plaster work. The scheme featured a series of heraldic shields of the Constable lineage. Plaster figures were also commissioned by William; a number of these supplied by sculptor John Cheere (1709-1787). Prominently placed above the fireplace was a carving of oak boughs and garlands , crowned by the Garter Star.

Domenico Bartoli, working at Burton Constable, 1763-1766, on an annual salary of 52 guineas, was responsible for the four scagiola table tops in the Great Hall.

Formerly the Parlour in the 16th century house, the room was extensively remodelled under William Constable in the 1760s. Once more Timothy

The Staircase

Lightoler won the design commission against stiff opposition. The notion of 'good eating leads to good health' is a theme reflected in a number of ways in the room and is quite appropriate for its purpose.

The ceiling takes inspiration from a classical design; Italian stuccoist Giuseppe Cortese (fl. 1725-1778), based in York, undertook the plasterwork. Hull's Jeremiah Hargrave carved the door cases, side tables and pedestals for the sculpture. The life-size figure of Bacchus was undertaken by William Collins for the sum of 16 guineas in January 1768. The dining table and chairs are by John Lowry and dated 1768.

Initially there was a modest staircase in the Elizabethan house, then a more elaborate one by the late 16th century. The present cantilevered staircase is another of Lightoler's designs and dates from the 1760s. Hanging at the foot of the staircase are three copies of noted paintings which were executed after William Constable completed his Grand Tour. These include reproductions of works by Guido Reni and Titian.

provide a rare insight into how Brown executed his grand schemes at Burton Constable.

In 1773 Beverley plant grower Samuel Sigston provided 500 two-year old larches at 3 shillings a hundred; 100 elms 5-6 feet high for 20 shillings and 2000 beeches 9 feet tall. He was not the only supplier as William Constable also purchased trees from York, Chelsea, Holland, France and even America.

The Steward John Raines was in charge of the day-to-day running of the estate and oversaw all major works. During the 1760s and 1770s he was the person signing the receipts for payments. He met with Brown to survey the estate and recorded Brown's directions, which still survive today!

Hundreds of labourers were needed for excavating the lakes, felling trees, laying the new roads and countless other arduous tasks in order to create Brown's landscape. The exact labour numbers are not recorded in the accounts, as the overseeing workman would have paid them directly.

The Bridge

'Capability' Brown made eight visits to Burton Constable between 1772 and 1782 to landscape the park for William Constable. His visits took place in the Autumn and for each encounter the house steward recorded the minutes of the meetings under the headings 'Hints from Mr. Brown' and 'Mr. Brown's Directions'. The survival of these minutes

Straight lines and geometric patterns of 17th century Burton Constable's formal gardens were abandoned for the introduction of sinuously curving plantations of trees mirroring lakeside edges, woodland greeting the horizon and picturesque glimpses of the Hall through tree clumps.

Spectacular features of Brown's work at Burton Constable are the two serpentine lakes separated by a bridge. During his visit on 30th September 1775 it was recognised that in order to expand the lake, whilst maintaining the appearance of a single piece of water, a Southern Lake adjoining the newly created North Lake would need to be separated by a dam. Brown proposed introducing a bridge as a clever means to disguise this.

Capabilty Brown worked right up to his death from a heart attack on February 6 1783 in London.

In 1784 William Constable boasted about his parkland improvements in a letter to his half-brother Marmaduke Tunstall: 'My park 40 years ago was 400 or 500 acres of a Wilderness of Old Thornes, old decayed forest trees, whins or gorse higher than a man on horseback, rushes, hillcocks, deep ridge and furrow, rivers and swamps and full of all kinds of game. Now all are removed at great expense.'

William Constable's companion for most of his life was his sister, and when she died in 1774, he married Catherine Langdale (1730-1804). Dying without issue, his estates passed in 1791 to his two nephews Edward (1750-1803) and then Francis Sheldon (1752-1821). Each one in turn adopted the Constable surname.

Neither brother had a surviving son when Francis Sheldon died, so Burton Constable passed briefly to a cousin, Sir Thomas Hugh Clifford (1762-1823) who assumed the additional name of Constable. His son Sir Thomas Aston Clifford Constable was only 17 when he succeeded to the Burton Constable estate and for a short period lived at the family home at Tixall.

Sir Clifford, as he was known, married his cousin Marianne Chichester (1800-62) and they subsequently moved to Burton Constable bringing along Marianne's sister Eliza (1798-1859). They extensively refurbished the house and for a number of years the building came alive with musical soirees and theatrical evenings.

During the 1830s London lamp manufacturer, William Collins (c.1803-1852) was responsible for supplying the Great Hall's central lantern and other lanterns and lamps within the house. A group of life-size ancestral portraits formerly hanging in the Gallery were transferred to the Great Hall.

The Dining Room was redecorated and the walls, once painted pink, were covered in green by Wright & Dreyer of Hull. Additional gilding was applied to the decorative plasterwork and carved wood work. A number of paintings were brought to Burton Constable from Tixall in the 1840s. Included was the enormous picture, *Corialanus*, which hangs above the staircase.

The Gallery which had been completed by the close of the 16th century and modernised in the late 17th century was given a new elaborate decorative plasterwork ceiling and frieze. Also installed was an assortment of early stained glass from the dismantled chapel at Tixall. Whilst Sir Clifford and wife Marianne had honeymooned in Rome they bought some sphinx tables by Giuseppe Leonardi (fl. 1781-1811) with marble tops by the mosaicist Giacomo Raffaelli (1753-1836) and these found space in the Gallery.

The Gallery

Perhaps one of the most significant developments in this period was the establishment of the Chinese Room. Once used as William Constable's Lodging Room, as he slipped into old age in the 1780s, the room was created after Marianne and her sister Eliza acquired inspiration from visits to Brighton Pavilion during the late 1820s. New Chinese wallpaper was hung on the walls and stencilled designs added to doors and walls. Thomas Brooks (1778-1850) carved the gilded dragons positioned on either side on the window bay. An elaborate dragon chair, designed by Marianne was carved in 1841 by Thomas Ward of Hull.

The Chinese room

When Marianne died, Sir Clifford married his mistress Rosina Brandon (1833-1908). Until his death in 1870, cash was lavishly spent on both Burton Constable and Dunbar House, their villa at Teddington in Middlesex. Sir Clifford's son, Sir Frederick Augustus Talbot (1828-1894) never lived at Burton Constable and produced no legitimate heir.

In 1894 the Burton Constable estates passed through the female line (via Thomas Hugh Clifford's daughter Mary Barbara) to the Chichesters of Devon and Ireland. Under Lt. Col. Walter Raleigh Chichester Constable (1863-1942) and his wife Edith Smyth-Pigot, the house enjoyed extensive refurbishment following the couple's move there in 1900.

Furnishings removed by Sir Thomas Aston Clifford Constable's second wife Rosina, around the time of his death, were returned to Burton Constable, from her home in Italy, when she died in 1908.

Financial constraints in the 1930s forced the Chichesters to leave Burton Constable Hall and relocate to a smaller property on the estate, Wood Hall. The Lt Colonel's son, Brigadier Raleigh Chichester Constable (1890-1963) and his family moved back to Burton Constable Hall after the Second World War.

The Brigadier's son John Chichester Constable (1927-2011) along with his wife Gay (1935-1989) were determined to secure the future of Burton Constable and its collections. After negotiations between the Chichester Constable family, the National Heritage Memorial Fund and Leeds City Council, the Burton Constable Foundation was established in March 1992.

Burton Constable and its parkland presently belongs to the Burton Constable Foundation, while descendants of the family still own the surrounding estate and also occupy the house's South Wing.

View from the east, 2016.

Cannon Hall

An engraving of the Hall viewed from the Lake

Mrs Fraser Spencer-Stanhope as a young girl

The 300 year occupancy of the stately home Cannon Hall, near Cawthorne, west of Barnsley, by the Spencer-Stanhope family came to an abrupt halt in 1951 when it was sold along with the 150-acre parkland to Barnsley Council. Mrs Fraser Spencer-Stanhope made the sale for £15,750 because of death duties and taxation. Prior to the sale, all the house's splendid contents were sold.

The Hall which had 50 rooms was intended to provide 28 flats for the Corporation. The park, sloping down from the Hall to the stream known as the Lesser Dearne, measured 150 acres.

The Council had received the formal consent of the Ministry of Local Government and Planning to borrow £3,200 repayable in 30 years, to purchase the Hall, and £7,550 repayable in 60 years for the purchase of the park lands. At a subsequent meeting of Barnsley Town Council, the acquisition of this important property brought no comment from members on either side of the Chamber.

Daughter of the Hon. John Montague Spencer-Stanhope, Mrs Spencer-Stanhope inherited Cannon

Servants at the Hall

Workmen outside the Hall front

The Drawing Room 1920

Hall on his death in 1944. She had married Rear Admiral, the Hon. George Fraser in 1921 but the marriage was dissolved in 1934. Afterwards she was granted Royal Licence to use the surname and coat of arms of the Spencer-Stanhope family. On selling the Hall and park she lived at Banks Hall, Cawthorne.

Mrs Spencer-Stanhope's obituary in 1964 said she was an unassuming individual. She was the last of the line of Spencer-Stanhopes at Cannon Hall, had been extremely active in Cawthorne village affairs and many other philanthropic causes. Among her many activities and interests were membership of the Parish Council from 1946 and of the Parochial Church Council from 1944. She was President of the Women's section of the Penistone Division Conservative Association and of the Cawthorne Association.

Barnsley Corporation acquired Cannon Hall, in the face of stiff competition from several influential sources. Sheffield Regional Hospital Board wanted the Hall to serve as a hospital.

In 1954, art lovers and conservationists probably breathed a sigh of relief when Mayor of Barnsley Alderman A. E. McVie, speaking at the annual exhibition of the Barnsley & District Art Society, proudly announced Barnsley Corporation had decided to convert Cannon Hall into an Art Gallery and Museum, instead of flats. The original intention was turned down by the Ministry of Housing and Local Government. The Mayor said that the council were encouraged to buy Cannon Hall as the result of the successful scheme of converting Wentworth Castle, Stainborough, another local mansion, into a teachers' training college. The Corporation was advised on the lay-out of the whole place by Mr E.I. Musgrave, director of Leeds City Art Gallery and Temple Newsam House. He gave the Corporation a comprehensive report on the Hall and grounds,

Cannon Hall, with its gardens and over 70 acres of unspoilt, well-wooded parkland was opened to the public in 1957. In the Hall's Ballroom the Earl of Scarbrough officiated at the opening ceremony before an invited audience. The chairman of the Estates Committee, Coun. Fred Elliott. presided at the ceremony, and the Mayor of Barnsley, Coun. S. Jubb, moved a vote of thanks to Lord Scarbrough.

Seven of the principal rooms had been re-decorated and furnished in appropriate period style under the guidance of first curator, Alister Campbell.

'What the public will see is only the first part of the

First Cannon Hall curator Alister Campbell

development programme for the museum', Mr Campbell said. 'Eventually the greater part of the Hall will be opened to the public and it is intended to use rooms on the first floor to house travelling exhibitions of art. The building up of a museum worthy of the town will of necessity be a slow process. We mean to set a high standard,' he said.

Most of the exhibits were loaned or given by public spirited benefactors. The Earl of Yarborough, for example, had loaned many fine exhibits from Brocklesby Park. These included a set of eight Gobelin tapestry panels woven with designs depicting cherubs symbolic of the arts and science, two sets of Louis XV armchairs and sofas upholstered in Aubusson tapestry.

The Earl of Coventry had loaned amongst other things, a set of eight armchairs designed by Robert Adam for Croome Court, the home of the Earl of Derby. Mrs Fraser Spencer-Stanhope loaned a number of items connected with the Hall. These included a number of pieces of Greek and Roman Statuary. The National Art Collection Fund gave a magnificent Mortlake tapestry, a set of Chippendale chairs from the Cook collection. A grant by the NACF was given towards the purchase by the Barnsley Corporation of a portrait of Lady Houblon by Lely.

Shortly after the opening one anonymous writer to a local newspaper said they were not convinced that 'Barnsley could afford the luxury of having its own country house museum when money is short and there are other matters requiring attention in the town...On my visit I found little over which I could enthuse and nothing that would attract me to make a second or third visit'. This criticism however was very premature.

A house of some description had existed on the Cannon Hall site since the 13th century and was owned by Gilbert Canun who is alleged to have inspired its name. However, the first mention of the actual word Cannon was nearby 'Cannon Grove', wood from which fuelled local iron smelting in the early 1300s. Eventually, the house passed into the hands of the Bosvilles.

John Spencer (1719-1776)

In 1650 Sir William Hewitt sold a manor, farm and 'capital messuage named Cannon Hall' to Robert Hartley for £2,900. A few years later it was acquired by John Spencer of Montgomeryshire (died in 1681) who arrived in Cawthorne before 1660. The Spencer family had Royalist loyalties and this may have been a main reason for them relocating. Spencer bought the Hall from his step-daughter, Margaret, after she had inherited it from her father, Robert Hartley.

This began the Spencer-Stanhope family's long association with Cannon Hall and in subsequent years the property was rebuilt and remodelled. Additionally, the family became a leading force in Barnsley's iron and coal industries developing a huge and wealthy empire. Following John's death the estate passed to his son also called John (d.1729) and then to his son William Spencer (d.1756). William married Christiana, an heiress from a rich Hathersage family. He had inherited £14,000 from her father in 1725. It is tempting to suggest this, perhaps, financed some of the construction work at Cannon Hall.

A tall central section to the Hall was constructed around the start of the 18th century and may have been designed by architect John Etty; the interiors by local craftsman John Thornton.

A dark side to the family was that one of William's sons, Benjamin ran a slave-trading ship – *The Cannon Hall*. An account by a representative in Antigua, said that some of 'the slaves were landed in a very weak and low condition..two of them died after being landed not being in a condition to be exposed to sale'.

Confidently, William claimed in his will that he had left nothing for his eldest son and heir John Spencer to do to the house.

Obviously disagreeing, John (1719-1776), from around the mid 18th century, employed York architect John Carr (1723-1807) to undertake major improvements which stretched over 30 years.

The cost was in the region of £30,000 (over £4 million today). Between 1764-1768, two single storey wings were added on the ends of the old Hall. Included was the Dining Room, designed to demonstrate the prosperity and sophistication of the family, and at its head John Spencer. The moulded ceiling is decorated in the Rococo style and the

The Library. [Barnsley Archives]

The Dining Room. [Barnsley Archives]

carved decoration of the door, window architraves, the dado panelling and window shutters are all original. A Neo-Classical fireplace reflects the influence of Italian architect Andrea Palladio.

After this work was undertaken, the rooms in the now central section of the Hall were remodelled, again by Carr, in 1778. He also moved the 17th century oak staircase leading to the upper floors to its current position. The upstairs rooms were occupied by the family; the servants had rooms in the attic.

The parkland evolved along with the Hall and from 1757 some of the finest surveyors, and landscape gardeners – including Richard Wood and Capability Brown – gave their thoughts on how to create a spectacular setting for the remodelled property.

Never marrying, John Spencer's heir was his sister Anne's son, Walter Stanhope (b.1750), and he inherited Cannon Hall in 1775. Thereafter, he changed his surname to Spencer-Stanhope by Royal Licence.

Educated at Bradford Grammar School, Walter studied at University College, Oxford and the Middle Temple, London. He was elected MP for Carlisle in 1775; Haslemere, 1780; Hull, 1784; Cockermouth, 1800; and for Carlisle, 1802. He was

Walter Spencer-Stanhope (1750-1821)

Sir Walter Spencer-Stanhope (1827-1911), seated in carriage

The Ballroom fireplace

a close supporter of William Pitt the Younger and friend of William Wilberforce, the anti-slavery campaigner who was a frequent visitor to Cannon Hall.

Walter campaigned against cruelty to animals in the name of sport and banned bull-baiting and cock-fighting on his land. Walter and his wife produced 15 children and perhaps out of practical necessity architect John Carr was asked to prepare designs for second storeys to the Hall's two wings. These were added in 1803-04.

Next in line to the Cannon Hall estates after Walter's death in 1821 was his second son John Spencer-Stanhope (b.1787-1873).

He matriculated at Christ Church, Oxford in 1804 and then after studying the ancient battlefields of Greece was captured in Barcelona by the French and imprisoned between 1810-1813. Napoleon I personally agreed for him to be freed. In time he published some of his Greek research. Illustrations were provided by his travelling companion, the architect and artist Thomas Allason.

John became a fellow of both the French Geographical Society and the Royal Society. With his wife, Lady Elizabeth (1795-1873), daughter of Thomas Coke of Norfolk, 1st Earl of Leicester, they had six children: Walter; John Roddam; Anna Maria; Louisa Elizabeth; Eliza Anne; and Anne Alicia.

John Roddam was a major artist who worked under the Pre-Raphaelite influence. He was associated with Edward Burne-Jones and George Frederick Watts. After initially working at Hillhouse, Cawthorne, he eventually moved to Florence.

Following John's death on November 8, 1873, Sir Walter Spencer-Stanhope (1827-1911) took hold of the Cannon Hall reins. Walter married Elizabeth Julia Buxton and they had 11 children. During their

The North Front

lifetime Cannon Hall was nicknamed 'Roast Beef Hall' because the couple hosted many prestigious events attended by a number of prominent guests. Walter also led an active public life becoming Deputy Lieutenant and a Justice of the Peace of the West Riding. He was knighted in 1904.

Walter's daughter Gertrude Spencer-Stanhope was a sculptor and painter in the Pre-Raphaelite style while another daughter Cecily helped create the unique 'Fairylands' within the grounds of Cannon Hall.

His niece Evelyn (daughter of sister Anna Maria) was another Pre-Raphaelite artist known by her married surname Evelyn De Morgan whose husband was the artist William De Morgan.

Entrance Hall c. 1920

John Montague Spencer-Stanhope (1860-1944)

The Landing c. 1920

Polish soldiers at the Hall

There was a major addition in 1891 when Sir Walter added an oak-panelled Ballroom to the Hall. Daughter Cecily may have been involved with the design which imitates a Jacobean Great Hall from the early 17th century. All the panelling lining the walls, the floor boards and the gallery itself was made by the estate carpenters. The splendid fireplace mantel piece came from Florence. Also built around the same time were the Victorian Kitchens and Servants' quarters.

Sir Walter died in 1911 and was succeeded by his son and heir, John Montague Spencer-Stanhope (1860-1944). He married Ida Mary Pilkington (1864-1920) and their only offspring was Margaret Elizabeth Ida Spencer-Stanhope (known locally as Miss Betty), who later sold Cannon Hall to Barnsley Council.

*Miss Betty, the last Spencer-Stanhope
to reside at Cannon Hall*

John Montague's time at Cannon Hall was much more sedate than when occupied by his predecessors. The turmoil of two world wars, widespread social unrest and considerable questioning of the social strata, was not a period when over indulgence in life's luxuries and benefits would have been appreciated.

During WWII the Cannon Hall estate was the home of land army girls, evacuees and American service men. After the cessation of hostilities Polish men and women; ex-servicemen and refugees found a temporary home on the estate.

During her last years at Cannon Hall and before the sale in 1951, Mrs Fraser Spencer-Stanhope lived with just a House Keeper and Butler for Company. In 1950, a plan was mooted by the Ministry of Power and Fuel to start open-cast mining near the Hall but thankfully was never implemented.

Under the ownership of Barnsley Council, Cannon Hall's collections have grown impressively. The first curator had the enviable task of creating a collection of fine and decorative art from scratch. His aim, and that which has driven Cannon Hall's curators ever since, was to display wonderful collections for the public's enlightenment and enjoyment.

Today, Cannon Hall houses an astounding mix of paintings, metalwork, ceramics, glassware and furniture collections. The Museum's collections are displayed in exhibition galleries and its historic rooms.

Touring exhibitions are regularly featured making the building a pleasure to visit time and time again, contradicting that anonymous critic's lack of enthusiasm all those years ago.

And, isn't it fitting, and a fine tribute to the Spencer-Stanhopes, that a fantastic collection of Evelyn De Morgan's paintings is on a five year sojourn at the Hall courtesy of the De Morgan Foundation.

HM The Queen at Cannon Hall on July 12, 1977. [YP]

Carlton Towers

'The simple late 18th century gates at the entry to the 250 acres of beautiful parkland are no preparation for the sensational late 19th century Gothic house which greets the visitor round the bend in the drive,' reads the first line of the Carlton Towers brochure. The impressive building, completed in the early 1870s, could have been even more overwhelmingly Gothic if the full spectacular plans had been carried out.

The Gothic Revival style in architecture was one of the most influential of the 19th century. Exponents sought to revive medieval Gothic architecture, perhaps as a rebellion against neo-classical styles around at the time. Inherent in Gothic Revival are certain features, derived from buildings of the 12th to 16th centuries and amongst these are: pointed arches, steep-sloping roofs, decorative tracery, finials, scalloping, lancet windows and hood mouldings.

Art critic Kenneth Clarke writing of the movement said: 'It changed the face of England, building and restoring churches all over the countryside, and filling our towns with Gothic banks and grocers, Gothic lodging houses and insurance companies, Gothic everything from a town hall to a slum public house...'

The Gothic Revival movement was also intertwined with deeply philosophical and religious ideas, with serious study combined with a more fanciful, romantic vision of medieval chivalry and romance.

At the time of the Domesday Survey, Carlton was held, along with 93 other Yorkshire manors, by Robert de Brus. Over the ensuing centuries, the manors were subdivided. On Peter de Brus' death in 1268, Carlton passed to his sister Laderine and her husband John de Bellew. When he died in 1301, Carlton was inherited by Nicholas Stapleton, his powerful family originating from Stapleton-on-Tees, near Darlington, Richmondshire. William the Conqueror had granted the village and the surrounding area to a knight who became known as Benedict de Stapleton.

From Nicholas Stapleton, Carlton passed to his nephew Sir Brian in 1374 and then to his grandson also called Brian (c.1385-1418). The latter is noted as the first of the family to live there in a house on the estate from 1394 and this became his principal seat. Nothing visible remains of the property and there is no documentary evidence.

Around 1476, one of a succession of Brian

An 18th century view of Carlton Hall

Carlton Hall after alterations undertaken by the 8th Lord Beaumont in 1842

Stapletons of Carlton married Joan Lovell, the niece and co-heiress of the last Viscount Beaumont. This made the Stapletons heirs to the barony of Beaumont, a barony in fee which was inheritable through the female line. The last English titles in fee were created at the coronation of Richard II in 1377 and later English titles are entailed on male heirs only. The barony of Beaumont title was not, however, re-claimed by the family for over 300 years.

In 1614, a three-storey square block was built at Carlton becoming known as Carlton Hall by Elizabeth, widow of Richard Stapleton and granddaughter of Bess of Hardwick.

It is speculated the building may even retain some of the masonry of the medieval house of the Stapletons which occupied the same site on a sandbank above the flood level of the River Aire. The three-storey structure forms the core of the existing house.

The first major changes to the house occurred following Thomas Stapleton's inheritance of the property in 1750. John Martin Robinson in *A Catalogue of the Architectural Drawings at Carlton Towers, Yorkshire* mentions Thomas Stapleton's first change was to abolish the original entrance in the middle of the West Front which opened into a Screens Passage and Great Hall. Instead, he built in brick 'a five bay wing to the to the north with a central canted bow window containing a new entrance. A Dining Room with Corinthian columns and a carved wooden chimney-piece was created from the old Hall and Screens Passage'.

Robinson adds: 'The architect has not been identified and no drawings survive today for this first stage of the eighteenth-century remodelling'.

In considering rearranging the parkland Thomas Stapleton initially consulted leading landscape gardener Richard Woods who produced a design in 1765. This was not accepted and Thomas White's ideas were adopted instead. His work included a large lake, wooded walks, a long drive from the house and a walled garden.

Designs for further alterations to Carlton Hall were supplied by Thomas Atkinson (1729-1798), the most notable being the rebuilding of the stables c.1777 (the date recorded on the clock) and the addition of a Catholic Chapel.

In 1794, Thomas Stapleton made an unsuccessful claim to the dormant barony of Beaumont. The matter was referred to the Committee of Privileges and the claim was allowed in 1840, when his great nephew Miles Thomas Stapleton, was called to the House of Lords as the 8th Lord Beaumont.

After his enoblement, Miles Thomas Stapleton, 8th Lord Beaumont, was inspired to undertake further remodelling of the house though no drawings exist.

He converted the 1777 East Wing, extending nearly 200 feet, into part of the house, Gothicising the exterior and converting the Chapel into a connecting series of state rooms with the new rooms behind. He was probably his own architect and the result was not successful. Robinson (*op.cit.*) mentions the style adopted was 'an uninspired Gothic with cement battlement red and blue carpets woven with heraldic lions, wallpapers patterned with gold fleurs de lys, and an interesting collection of specially manufactured antiquities including "ancient" armour, masses of old oak and two brand new sets of "Charles I" chairs'.

Not surprisingly, his son Henry, 9th Lord Beaumont, eventually decided to remodel the whole house some years after his inheritance in 1854.

Henry, born at Carlton Hall in 1848, was educated at Eton, and joined the 1st Life Guards from September 1868 until December 1869 when he bought himself out. After a visit to Rome he converted to Roman Catholicism aged around 21. Described as an impetuous man, he was fond of romantic gestures and acted on various outlandish ideas as they struck him. For example, in 1870 he rushed off to serve on the staff of the Prussian Crown Prince in the Franco-Prussian War. The King of Bavaria made him a Knight of the Grand Cross of the Holy Sepulchre.

Henry Stapleton, 9th Lord Beaumont

E.W. Pugin's design for enlarging Carlton Hall, 1873

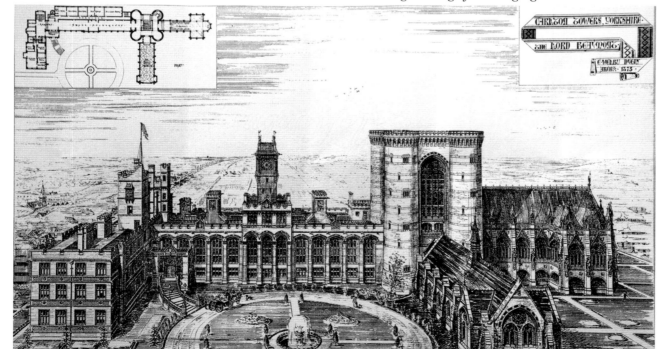

During the early 1870s he began the megalomaniac Gothic transformation of Carlton and employed Edward Welby Pugin (1834-1875) to produce designs. Edward was the son of the more famous Augustus Welby Northmore Pugin (1812-1852), often referred to as 'God's Architect', due to the large number of ecclesiastical designs he produced.

The Venetian Drawing Room

The Picture Gallery

Pugin snr had a major influence on the style and theory of the Gothic Revival urging architects and designers to work from the fundamental principles of Medieval art. Amongst his own work was the Palace of Westminster and numerous designs for furniture, metalwork, ceramics, textiles, stained glass and wallpaper. He also organised the Medieval Court display at the Great Exhibition of 1851.

His son's work at Carlton Hall included re-facing the exterior with cement to look like stone and adding the turrets, gargoyles, battlements and coat of arms innumerable, which seemingly justified the change of name from Carlton Hall to Carlton Towers.

Remodelling the old house was only half of Edward Pugin and Lord Beaumont's grand plans. Both men intended to extend the house to twice its present size as a surviving drawing by Pugin testifies. But, the proposed Grand Staircase, Chapel and Great Hall were never built. Both eccentrics, Beaumont and Pugin quarrelled whilst Carlton was still being built and the reason behind this is unknown.

Following the disagreement, a different, younger architect was called upon to design the interior. This was the Yorkshire-born John Francis Bentley. He was one of the leading church architects of the late 19th century and is best known for Westminster Cathedral. The rooms at Carlton are his only major country house commission. They are a complete contrast to Pugin's harsh exterior both in their sensitive, scholarly design and also in quality of craftsmanship. Completion took approx. 15 years.

Edward Pugin eventually ruined his career by expensive and unnecessary litigation trying to prove that his father, and not Sir Charles Barry, had designed the Houses of Parliament. He died in 1875 around the time Carlton was complete although the combination of Pugin, Bentley and other 'speculations', left Lord Beaumont with a debt of over £250,000.

Rooms on the ground floor which range from the cosy to the opulent include the Bow Drawing Room, Armoury, Inner Hall, Venetian Drawing Room, Card Room and Picture Gallery. The Venetian Drawing Room (occupying the former site of the 18th century Private Chapel) is undoubtedly one of the house's finest rooms. Bentley took inspiration for his designs from discovering some old Venetian glasses in a cupboard and arranged the room with cabinets in the dado to display them. Other features are the dado panels painted by N.H.J. Westlake; the upper parts of the walls covered in moulded plaster with a pattern of pomegranates gilded to look like stamped leather; and the decorated cornice. Perhaps the room's most impressive feature is the chimneypiece adorned with heraldry and panels of Flora and the Four seasons by Westlake. William De Morgan provided the yellow embossed fireplace tiles.

The Armoury, sitting between the older part of the house and the wing of 1777, is decorated with carved oak panelling by J. Erskine Knox and stencilled painting on the ceiling.

Adjoining the Venetian Drawing Room, the Card Room was created out of the priest's lodgings. It features oak linen-fold panelling carved by J. Erskine Fox. Both the curtains and silver-plated chandelier were designed by Bentley.

Baroness Beaumont, 11th holder of the title

The Card Room

On 28th July 1888, he married Violet, daughter of Frederick Wootton Isaacson, MP. She had a fortune of £120,000, and Lord Beaumont had an annual income of £25,400 from lands in Yorkshire, London and Dover. Yet, even with all this cash, a greater part of the estates had to be sold in 1888-89 – in Yorkshire the five thousand seven hundred acres were reduced to two thousand, in London and Dover the lands went altogether, mainly to reduce outstanding debts. The couple had no children and Lord Beaumont died of pneumonia in 1892.

Pictured in 1978 are the 17th Duke of Norfolk, KG and his son, Edward, 18th Duke of Norfolk, 5th Lord Howard of Glossop and 13th Baron Beaumont. [YP]

In subsequent years, Lord Beaumont served as a captain in the army of Don Carlos, helping him with his claim for the Spanish throne. Beaumont was later appointed Carlist representative in England where he signed himself "Chargé D´ Affaires, Spécial et Officieux, of H.M. Charles VII." In 1879 he served with the 17th Lancers in Zululand and he was present at the Battle of Ulundi.

Much of the remainder of his life was spent abroad, yet he must have made periodic visits to Carlton because the game-books show that he shot 1,644 partridges in the season 1884-85 and 1,903 in the following season.

The Jacobean section of the house is on the right. [YP]

Tragically, the 10th Lord Beaumont shot and killed himself in an accident during 1895. The barony passed through the female line to Josephine Tempest Stapleton, becoming 11th Baroness Beaumont. She married Bernard Fitzalan-Howard, 3rd Lord Howard of Glossop, great-grandson of the 13th Duke of Norfolk, and owned Carlton for 76 years.

She and her husband were one of the few couples to both hold titles in their own right. They had eight children.

During the WWII, Carlton Towers was occupied as a military hospital and was restored thereafter.

Following the death of the Baroness in August 1971, her eldest son Miles Francis Stapleton Fitzalan Howard, inherited both the Beaumont and Howard of Glossop baronies, becoming the 12th Baron Beaumont. He married Anne Mary Constable-Maxwell and they had two sons and three daughters. One of them, Lord Gerald Fitzalan Howard lives at Carlton Towers with his wife and their children.

Over the past few decades Carlton Towers has been used for a number of film and TV settings including the 1988 film version of Evelyn Waugh's novel *A Handful of Dust*; and the TV series *Micawber* starring David Jason. The South Australian Film Corporation also used the house in the film *Like Minds* (2006).

Aerial view, 2010. [YP]

Castle Howard

Sometimes unusual liaisons between individuals can create remarkable results. This was true when Charles Howard, 3rd Earl of Carlisle, met John Vanbrugh and they built Castle Howard, regarded as the foremost country house in Yorkshire and amongst the most spectacular in the country.

Charles Howard, Castle Howard's patron, was born in 1669 at Naworth, close to Hadrian's Wall. Educated at Morpeth Grammar School, he married at the age of 19, Lady Anne Capel, daughter of the first Earl of Essex, who was only 13 at the time. But, it was claimed that 'through the greenness of their years [they] do not yet cohabit together'.

A few months after the wedding, Charles, initially Viscount Morpeth, embarked on the standard mode of cultural education for the nobility, the Grand Tour of Europe. Although exact details of his itinerary are unknown, it is assumed that he spent time in Holland, then Germany, Vienna, Venice, Padua and Rome. Whilst abroad he kept note books which contain details of what he saw and read about artists such as Raphael, Holbein and Titian. He also noted details of important families in Rome besides information of contemporary artists.

He took his Grand Tour seriously, absorbing all he could about art, antiquities and undoubtedly making opinions about architecture to nurture future unique ideas of his own.

Returning to England in February, 1691, he became 3rd Earl of Carlisle in April, 1692 on the death of his father. From 1695, he spent time away from the north east, at his London property (Carlisle House) in Soho Square. He moved in fashionable court society as well as developing a keen interest in political matters. He demonstrated an affinity to the political principles of the Whigs.

Towards the end of the century he adorned Carlisle House with works of art and sculpture. He commissioned a painting to decorate the ceiling of the main staircase, and collected china, delftware furniture and large numbers of books. For all these items and projects he spent large amounts of cash.

During July 1698, he journeyed to Henderskelfe, north east of York, which contained a medieval castle once owned by his grandfather and that had seen

Portrait of the 3rd Earl by William Aikman, painted in 1728, reproduced courtesy of Castle Howard

improvements during the 1680s but had burned down in 1693. In October 1698 he took out a lease for life on the Castle and Manor of Henderskelfe from his grandmother.

By May 1699, he had grandiose plans in mind for building on the Henderskelfe area the projected Castle Howard. The question of why he decided to build on such a grand scale is supposedly unknown. Yet, Charles Saumarez Smith in *The Building of Castle Howard* (1990) offers several considered explanations. Firstly, the author claims the Earl might have harboured a desire to glorify the Howard family in the construction of a great house. Secondly, it is submitted that the Earl too wanted to be remembered. Around the time of the house's conception Lord Carlisle was enjoying power and prominence at Court.

A model of the proposed Castle Howard structure was shown to an enlightened King William III, fascinated by building and gardening, during June 1700. Days later Carlisle was appointed one of the Gentlemen of his Majesty's Bedchamber. Carlisle later went on the be member of the Privy Council.

In the years leading up to the construction of Castle Howard, particularly around the mid-17th century, country house building was restrained and unostentatious. By the 1680s a change was taking place with houses becoming more extravagant and monumental, symbolizing owners' power and social position. Amongst the houses were those at Thoresby in Nottinghamshire and particularly Chatsworth in Derbyshire and Petworth in Sussex, all setting a new high standard in the country gentleman's exclusive world. This new confidence undoubtedly further inspired and underpinned the Earl of Carlisle's desire to embark on his own colossal house project.

By March 1699, architect William Talman, who was a pupil of Sir Christopher Wren, had been invited to

Sir John Vanbrugh

make drawings for Carlisle's new house. Having been involved with work at Chatsworth House and built up a reputable practice which enjoyed Royal patronage, Talman was considered to be the man for the Castle Howard job.

Unfortunately, his preliminary drawings were not deemed grandiose enough for the Earl of Carlisle's visions. Also, Talman, by reputation, was a very awkward character and it is suspected there may have been a fall out with the Earl over costs, all this conspiring to make the architect loose the commission.

The Earl of Carlisle then turned to one of his chums in the Kit-Kat Club, Captain John Vanbrugh, to produce the house plans. Vanbrugh had no qualifications or prior experience for such a mighty task only boundless enthusiasm for art, literature and architecture.

Vanbrugh was baptised in London during January 1664 but grew up in Chester. After undertaking various positions at home and abroad he took up an army commission in 1686.

A radical throughout his life, he was arrested in Calais during 1688 for voicing support for William of Orange and was imprisoned there until April 1691. From February 1692 he was held in the Bastille and was subsequently allowed to roam around Paris (but not leave the country), admiring and studying French comic drama as well as much of the new architecture.

Quite a number of the designs he saw in the French capital, including Louis Le Vau's College des Quatre Nations and Jules Hardouin's-Mansart's chateau and Marly, were later doubtlessly discussed with the Earl of Carlisle and re-emerged in the plans for Castle Howard.

Returning to Britain in April 1693, Vanbrugh joined the Navy and then exchanged a military life for London and the London stage. A committed Whig, Vanbrugh, as a member of the Kit-Kat Club, was well-liked for his enormous geniality, his great humour and easy-going temperament. Other members of the Club at this time included many artists, writers, and noted gentlemen.

Towards the end of the 1690s Vanbrugh produced his first theatrical comedy, *The Relapse, or Virtue in Danger* (1696); and another play *The Provoked Wife* (1697). More robust, even more immoral than those of such contemporaries as William Congreve, Vanbrugh's plays were often attacked by critics.

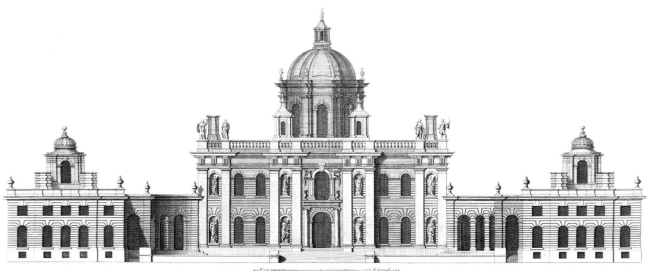

The Front to the Court of Castle Howard. Design'd by S.r I. Vanbrugh K.t
Elevation du Chateau D'Howard du costé de la Cour.

The north elevation of the house from Vitruvius Britannicus.

Castle Howard copperplate engraving from Vitruvius Britannicus.

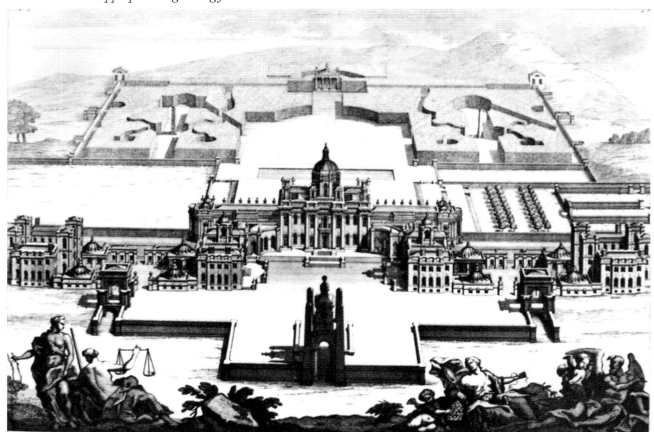

Carlisle was impressed by Vanbrugh's general enthusiasm. He put his confidence in the playwright transferring his skills to architecture and awarded him the commission for designing Castle Howard which would face north-south.

The proposal was discussed amongst Carlisle's friends and associates of the Kit-Kat Club suggesting a healthy interest in architecture and a support network when experimentation was being undertaken and critical analysis sought.

Vanbrugh made visits to a number of English houses before beginning his designs and amongst them were the Earl of Nottingham's, Burley-on-the-Hill and, naturally, Chatsworth House. Work on the Castle Howard foundations began in 1701 and the later inclusion of a dome to the design was applauded as adding visual excitement to the house.

The untrained Vanbrugh was helped greatly by Nicholas Hawksmoor, the very competent clerk of Sir Christopher Wren. Although often seen as adopting an assistant role, Hawksmoor was in effect indispensible to Vanbrugh and his equal partner in devising Castle Howard, which became renowned as a peak in English Baroque design.

William Etty from York was clerk of works on the project, the masons included William Smith, John Elsworth and a Major Smith. Work began first on the East Wings of both the Entrance Front and the Garden Front; the mason's tasks being completed by the autumn of 1702 and the summer of 1703 respectively. Internal fittings on the garden front structure were carried out during 1705/6.

Excavations for the main block of the house – including the Saloon and Hall – began once work in the two other areas was well-advanced. It began to take on a finished appearance by the summer of 1706. From the autumn of the previous year, a French Huguenot carver, Mr Nadauld or Nedos was involved in producing decorations inside and outside of the house. He had previously been employed at Hampton Court and Chatsworth and received payment of over £844 for his Castle Howard work.

As construction was nearing completion on the main block, work began on the West Wing of the Garden

View of the South Parterre, painted by William Marlow in the 1770s, reproduced courtesy of Castle Howard

Front. Then, instead of construction moving to the West Wing of the Entrance Front, which was to include a Chapel, the masons started on structures and a courtyard to the east of the Kitchen Wing. Thus, the Castle Howard exterior was complete towards the end of 1709.

Charles Saumarez Smith (*op. cit.*) states the third Earl of Carlisle kept meticulous accounts on the building of Castle Howard: '...Lord Carlisle would twice annually examine detailed accounts which he required to be sent to him and which he would approve only subject to comments and corrections. If there was any mistake, he would spot it'.

In appraising Carlisle's income and expenditure, Smith concludes financing the building of Castle Howard must have been a struggle for the Earl, particularly following his dismissal from the post as First Lord of the Treasury upon the death of William III in March 1702.

Thus, to use finances stringently, the house was built in stages and materials used economically in certain areas of the building, yet maximised in others.

Rooms in the house started to be furnished from 1706 when textiles were ordered for several private rooms on the South Front. As time went by other textile furnishings – some rather exotic – as well as furniture were sent north usually from noted London suppliers.

Remarkable features incorporated into the house's interior occurred in 1709 when Lord Carlisle commissioned Gianantonio Pellegrini and Marco Ricci to produce paintings. Pellegrini decorated the staircase walls, pendentives and dome of the Great Hall; Ricci a series of genre scenes for the overdoors.

Within the Hall's dome, rising some 70ft into the air, was a painting of the 'Fall of Phaeton'; the pendentives included representations of the four elements, air, fire, earth and water. Pellegrini worked at Castle Howard roughly between 1709-1712, and amongst his other work was the ceiling of the ground floor Saloon and the High Saloon. Sadly, much of his artistic endeavour was lost in the fire of 1940. Ricci's work includes two surviving paintings: 'The Rehearsal of an Opera' and 'The Mall, St James's Park'.

With Castle Howard's interior decoration nearing the final stages by 1712 the rooms were supplied with furniture. There is little evidence about what

The Long Gallery. [YP]

Castle Howard, Temple of the Four Winds. [YP]

this initially comprised or how it was sourced but a probate inventory, compiled after the death of the 4th Earl of Carlisle (1694-1758) reveals a wide range of styles and materials present over the first 50 years of the house's existence.

Thoughts of how the grounds might appear were in Carlisle's mind from around 1699 when he asked leading garden designer and nurseryman of the time, George London for proposals. Renowned for his designs that owed much to French and Dutch influences, London's ideas were not what Carlisle had in mind. He wanted to adopt a more ambitious approach and one which embraced the surrounding landscape. It was to be the start of a new and different, more natural, kind of English gardening and took place at Castle Howard from around 1705.

London's rejected designs had proposed clearing the ancient Ray Wood to the east of the house. Instead, it was transformed into an exciting woodland garden that accommodated a number of architectural features, sculptures and a network of paths. Statues placed in the area included figures of Apollo, Bacchus and Neptune.

Castle Howard Mausoleum painted by Thomson and engraved by Hawksworth c. 1812

As attention continued to be concentrated on the landscape around the house there are records of extensive tree planting, many of them arriving from London by boat and landing at Scarborough or Bridlington.

In time, the parkland would be elaborated to include Vanbrugh's 'Temple of Diana' (later the 'Temple of the Four Winds') designed 1723/4 and Hawksmoor's 'Temple of Venus'. Amongst the other impressive structures in the landscape were Vanbrugh's Pyramid Gate, the great Obelisk (erected to commemorate the Duke of Marlborough's victories) and Hawksmoor's Mausoleum.

To carry out the work within the surrounding landscape, many buildings making up the small village of Henderskelfe were removed, amongst them being the medieval castle, houses, church and groups of smallholdings.

Regularly, Vanbrugh protested to Carlisle about completing the Entrance Front's West Wing but this was not started until the 1750s. By this time Vanbrugh had died in 1726 and the 3rd Earl in 1738.

The 3rd Earl spent much of his last years retired and out of public life. His achievements are aptly summed up by Dr Christopher Ridgway in *The Gardens at Castle Howard* (2010): '[Carlisle] succeeded in raising the most comprehensive monument possible: Castle Howard was an entire landscape fashioned in his name, which would dwarf the ephemeral glories of political life and last well beyond his lifetime'.

Under the direction of the 4th Earl, the West Wing was completed quite surprisingly to the Palladian designs of the 3rd Earl's son-in-law, Sir Thomas Robinson. This strongly contrasted with the Baroque appearance of the rest of the building.

Over the ensuing centuries the magnificent Castle Howard has remained with the Carlisle branch of the Howard family. For a brief period during WWII, the house became a girls school.

A major fire on November 9, 1940, starting in the south-east corner of the South Front, quickly swept in a westerly direction through the house. Destruction affected almost 20 rooms, amongst them were the Garden Hall, High South rooms and Cabinet Room. Perhaps the main casualty was the Great Hall's dome which collapsed. Thankfully, but over a long period of time, the dome and many of the destroyed rooms have been restored, although the south-east wing remains a shell.

The fire of November, 1940. [YP]

Castle Howard was opened to the public in 1952 and has provided a setting for a number of films and television series. The house became 'Brideshead' in the 1981 television serial and 2008 film adaptations of Evelyn Waugh's novel *Brideshead Revisited*.

The house is presently owned by Castle Howard Estate Ltd and run by Nicholas and Victoria Howard. In the past, according to the Castle Howard website, the Howard story was one of ambition, service, liberal politics and artistic endeavours.

'Today, above all, it is about the challenge of preserving the family home as a national treasure for family and visitors alike to enjoy,' states the website.

Major George Anthony Geoffrey Howard,
Baron Howard of Henderskelfe, (1920 –1984)
outside the house. [YP]

The Chapel, courtesy of Tony Bartholomew

The interior of the Chapel with The Hon Simon Howard, March 2014. [YP]

Cusworth Hall

Cusworth Hall, near Doncaster, was built by William Wrightson (b.1676). The building replaced an earlier house which formerly existed in the centre of the old Cusworth village and adjacent to the main road extending to Sprotbrough and Melton.

A suggestion of how the older house may have appeared is provided by a Samuel Buck 1720 sketch. This shows the building with five gables, yet a 1719 survey plan shows the Hall as a mere single block that includes an archway and courtyard.

The Wrightson family had been connected with Cusworth from 1669 when Robert Wrightson (b.1629), an attorney to the court of the King's Bench, acquired the Manor and Lordship of Cusworth, previously owned by the Wray family, from around 1560. The name Cusworth can be traced to the Domesday Survey of 1086.

Whilst living at Cusworth, Robert Wrightson undertook some improvements to the village in 1702 and when he died in 1708 left his estates to his eldest son (from a third marriage) Thomas Wrightson (b. 1674). It is to the latter gentleman that we are

William Wrightson, the builder of the new Cusworth Hall

indebted today for the superb maps he commissioned the celebrated surveyor/cartographer Joseph Dickinson to create of Cusworth. Before Thomas died in 1724 he was High Sheriff of Yorkshire.

Thomas was succeeded by his only brother William, who eventually built the new Cusworth Hall. Initially, William Wrightson resided in Newcastle with his wife Isabell, widow of a very wealthy coal

Samuel Buck sketch c. 1720, showing the old Cusworth Hall

The old Cusworth village

Before building commenced on the new classical style house there are records of William Wrightson making a number of improvements to the older property. He erected high walls to surround a number of areas and also built a Summer House in 1726.

However, these improvements did not satisfy him and he developed ideas for a much larger house and work on the foundations, according to the New House Accounts, was begun in March 1740. The design of the new house was entrusted to George Platt (1700-1743) born in Lyme Park, Cheshire, but settled in Rotherham by 1727 as a mason/architect. When George died in 1743 the project was allegedly taken over by his 16-year-old son, John who was later involved with building work at Wentworth Castle, Wentworth Woodhouse, Aston Hall and Clifton Hall.

Stone from quarries on the Cusworth estate was used to build the new house. Keen to keep a watch over the construction work, William reputedly gave daily instructions from a bosun's chair fastened to the scaffold.

Not long after the new, five-bay wide Central Hall was completed in 1745, William's son-in-law made

merchant and was elected Tory MP for the area in 1710. When defeated in the 1722 election, he subsequently stood for Northumberland and was victorious in 1723, but was forced to stand down the following year. This coincided with his brother's death and him succeeding to the Cusworth estate. His first wife had died some years earlier and he returned to Cusworth with a second wife, to run family affairs.

A view from the south, engraved by Thomas Malton

a comment that was to alter the building's general appearance. He claimed the Central Hall appeared 'too tall for its length' and as a result two wings were added to the designs of James Paine (1717-1789). Other work Paine was involved with in the Doncaster area was the town's Mansion House; Hickleton Hall; and Wadworth Hall. Of Paine's work at Cusworth, Nikolaus Pevsner, in *The Buildings of England: Yorkshire The West Riding* (1959) notes the architect's two added wings, then comments: 'He also altered the facade. It looks as if he did more'.

The two Cusworth added wings accommodated a Chapel, on the west side, and a Library on the east side. Craftsmen involved with work in the Hall included celebrated master plasterer, Joseph Rose (1745-1799) and artist Francis Hayman (1708-1776), formerly a student of William Hogarth. Hayman painted two pictures for the Chapel: 'The Good Samaritan' and 'The Ascension'. Pevsner (*op. cit.*) praises the work in the Chapel: 'The interior of the Chapel is sumptuous. Good plasterwork. Vaulted ceiling with penetrations and a big painting in the middle. The apse is separated from the rest by a Palladian opening, richly decorated'.

All the work on the new Cusworth Hall was completed around 1755 at a cost of around £20,000.

William Wrightson died in December, 1760 and his estate passed to his daughter Isabella and her husband John Battie of Warmsworth Hall, situated several miles away. William's only son, also called William, had died in infancy.

John Battie changed his name to John Battie Wrightson in 1761 and for much of his life he was involved in a quarrying business, situated near Sprotbrough along the navigable River Don.

During John Battie Wrightson's time at Cusworth he laid out the surrounding grounds, calling upon noted landscape gardener Richard Woods (1715 or 16-1793) to produce plans. Three of these survive with accompanying notes written as the project was being undertaken

His scheme, covering 100 acres, took five years to complete and included the construction of three lakes, formed from an existing stream named the Rose Dyke.

Dying at the relatively early age of 43, John Battie Wrightson was succeeded by his son William (b. 1752) who dropped the Battie part of his surname when 21. William's first wife died in 1782 two years after their marriage and with his second wife

Richard Heber Wrightson

produced five sons and three daughters.

William was Tory MP for Aylesbury between 1784-1790 and High Sheriff of Yorkshire 1818-1820. He died on Christmas Day 1827 and his eldest son William Battie Wrightson (b. 1789) inherited the Cusworth estates. Educated at Trinity College, Cambridge, he trained at Lincoln's Inn, being called to the Bar in 1815. William Battie Wrightson was elected MP for East Retford in 1826 and then sat for Hull from 1830 to 1832 and Northallerton from 1835 to 1865. He was at one time employed as a Commissioner of Inquiry into the state of the poor in Ireland. When he died without issue in February 1879, the Cusworth estates passed to his younger brother, Richard Heber Wrightson – then 79 years old.

The Heber part of his surname was taken from his mother's maiden name. He married twice but did not produce an offspring. On succeeding to the Cusworth estates he moved from Warmsworth Hall where he had lived for quite some time. In 1855 and 1890 Richard published two books, *History of Modern Italy* and *Sancta Republica Romana*.

On Richard Heber's death in 1891, the Cusworth estates were inherited by William Henry Thomas. His father was Charles Edward Thomas whose mother-in-law was Harriot, sister of William Battie Wrightson. Because Richard Heber had died childless, William Battie Wrightson had decreed,

William Henry Battie-Wrightson and Lady Isabella c. 1880

before his own death, that the Cusworth estates would pass to his nephew.

Born in 1855, William Henry Thomas attended Eton, and thereafter qualified as a barrister at Lincoln's Inn. Once he had inherited Cusworth, he took the name and arms of Battie-Wrightson by Royal Licence. In 1884 he married Isabella Georgiana Katherine Cecil, the eldest daughter of

William Henry Battie-Wrightson laid out in the Chintz Room shortly after his death

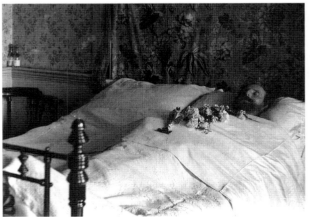

the third Marquis of Exeter. The couple lived at Warmsworth Hall and then at Cusworth Hall.

On April 28, 1903, Lady Isabella, or Her Ladyship as she was intermittently known, was deeply shocked, when her husband died suddenly of a cerebral haemorrhage, aged 47. While struggling to overcome her grief, she was involved with a legal wrangle with her husband's family. This was due to a clause which stated that on William Henry Battie-Wrightson's death, his son would inherit the Cusworth estates, only if he had reached the age of 21.

As Robert Cecil was only 15 in 1903, it was claimed by William Henry's brother, Charles Freeman Thomas, that Lady Isabella had no right to remain at Cusworth. But, after making an 'out of court' settlement, the matter was resolved.

Lady Isabella was known as quite a caring individual and on several occasions provided the poor and unemployed people of the area with food, opening soup kitchens in the grounds of Cusworth Hall. She organised the building of a new Dining Room behind the Chapel Wing in 1907. The addition was designed by Philip N. Brundell and constructed by

Robert Cecil Battie-Wrightson pictured in his Lieutenant's uniform.

Lady Isabella poses with her staff outside Cusworth Hall's north front c. 1910. She was providing refreshments for the King's Own Yorkshire Light Infantry

Lady Isabella (centre) is dressed as Britannia during a fancy dress party

View in the South Tapestry Room at the time of Robert Cecil's 21st birthday

the Doncaster firm of Grantham, Brundell & Farren.

Other domestic refinements such as electricity and a telephone were also installed in the Hall around this time. In Gordon Smith's *Cusworth Hall and the Battie-Wrightson Family* (1990) there is a useful plan of the Hall's ground floor said to show the layout during the early 20th century.

The north entrance led into the Square Hall Lounge; on the left side was the North Drawing Room; on

the right the Office. The Square Hall Lounge led to the Long Hall, giving access to the Tapestry Room, Book Room and Breakfast Room. The south east end of the Long Hall led to the Billiard Room Passage and the Billiard Room (former Library or Bow Room). The north west end of the Long Hall led to the Chapel Passage and in turn the Chapel and Dining Room.

Lady Isabella's son, Robert Cecil, took over the running of the Cusworth estates from the age of 21 in 1909, with Lady Isabella spending time away from Cusworth Hall. She stayed in the family's London properties and grace and favour residences, which included a villa she owned in Wothorpe.

During WWI, she converted the villa into a hospital and spent much of her time there running it. Whilst in Stamford on 26 October 1917 she caught a chill, which developed into pneumonia. Two days later she died aged 64 and was interred at Warmsworth cemetery alongside her late husband.

Robert Cecil had served as a lieutenant in the King's Own Yorkshire Light Infantry between 1907-1912. In 1914 he married Louie Evelyn Lupton and served during the Great War with the Royal Army Service Corps.

After the death of his mother and the cessation of hostilities 'he had little to do with the estate

View from the west of the South Front c. 1907. The new Dining Room is in the centre

management', said Gordon Smith in an article in *The Star* January 14, 1995. Gordon also added: 'It was fortunate that he had a good agent in R.J. Whittingham, who had been an employee for quite a while and kept the estate intact'.

Robert's wife left him when she discovered that he was having an affair with Christabel Bentley who moved into the Hall around 1930. Gordon believed that Robert was well-liked by the Hall staff. This was because he joined in with them at staff parties. They still knew that he was the boss, yet he didn't treat them like underlings and spoke to them courteously. During the summer some of the staff would accompany Robert to his residence at Felixstowe, where they stayed for four or five weeks.

Caring for Cusworth (n.d.), a book edited by Alison Morrish, recalls further memories of Robert's kindness to his staff: 'Birthdays were always celebrated and gifts were given for a Coming of Age. Edith Taylor remembers the gift being a gold wrist watch or chiming clock. Jessie Commons, on her 21st birthday, was sent home to invite her brother and sister to the Hall and returned to find the table set for tea, flowers and dancing, and two gold sovereigns from Mr Wrightson. On August Bank Holiday Monday a sports day was held and the staff could invite family and friends.'

Changes occurred at Cusworth during the WWII. Half the Hall was taken over by the military authorities. All the furnishings from the North Drawing Room, Billiard Room and Library were stacked ceiling-high in the main Tapestry Drawing Room. Furniture from the family's property in Portman Square, London, was moved to Cusworth and stacked in the chapel.

'After the war, the furniture was never moved back to its original place', said Gordon. 'It remained in a pile until Robert's death in 1952. If he confided in anybody in his later years, it was probably the agent Whittingham, who was a bit like a father figure to him. Don't forget, Robert was only 15 when he lost his father'.

Robert, who had never followed in his ancestors' footsteps, had lived his eccentric wayward life via finances drawn from the Cusworth Estate which, at the time of his death, was running at an annual loss of £3,000.

'This deficit was underpinned by capital taken from the family's stocks and shares and securities', explained Gordon.

He added: 'In previous years, the Battie-Wrightson's wealth was increased through marriage into landed families, lucrative occupations and executive appointments. Apart from being involved in local

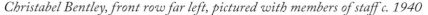

Christabel Bentley, front row far left, pictured with members of staff c. 1940

*Staff members: Clara Farr, Muriel Shaw and Lilian ?
take a dip in the lake*

cricket, Robert made no contributions to the family fortune. It was not only him that passed away on an April morning in 1952 it was also the ancient and unique Battie-Wrightson way of life, that had been perpetuated by generations and had existed for centuries'.

The Cusworth estates passed to Robert's sister, Barbara, known as Mrs Maureen Pearse, but he left £64,000 to his companion Christabel Bentley and £1,000 was paid to his servants. Death duties amounted to approx £280,000.

Gordon Smith (*op.cit.*) explains that securities of £250,000 were cashed but there was still a deficit. To meet this figure, Barbara decided to sell the Hall's contents at a sale held October 14-23, 1952.

At the sale was a 53-year-old restaurant owner from Milwaukee, Wisconsin and he commented to the *Yorkshire Post*, October 10, 1952: 'It's marvellously interesting but at the same time terribly depressing that all these possessions, carefully gathered together by a family over the years, should have to go in this way. In America we would take a place like this and turn it into a national monument'.

In the years following the sale, the empty Hall and grounds became a problem for Barbara. During 1955, there was an approach to turn the Hall into an old folks home; a plan in the same year proposed to build a prison nearby and use the Hall for administrative purposes. Barbara found both of these

unacceptable and in time the Prison Commissioners lost interest. Later, the Hall was leased to the Ivy Mount college which lasted for around 18 months. Doncaster Corporation put forward an idea to convert the Hall into a zoo, in May 1957 but this was strongly opposed by Barbara, who harboured a wish to have the building demolished but only if the Chapel could remain standing.

Towards the end of the 1950s just as Barbara's representatives were making a strong case to demolish the Hall, the Doncaster Rural District Council stepped in and bought the property and grounds for £7,500. Initially it was intended to turn the building into a hospital but this was abandoned in favour of establishing a museum.

Under the curatorship of well-known industrial historian, John Goodchild, Cusworth Hall opened as a museum in 1967. Initially, the focus was on industrial aspects of the local region but a switch was made when the Hall came under the auspices of the newly created Doncaster Metropolitan Borough Council in 1974. The museum's theme from around that time became South Yorkshire folk life.

The Children's Room May 25, 1992. [YP]

Duncombe Park

Britain's large country houses and estates were once the bedrock of a rural society. But they were wiped out in great numbers during the early 20th century through a variety of radical reasons: social, political, and most importantly, financial. This loss in certain instances came close to a social revolution as the local squire was depended upon to provide large-scale employment, housing and patronage to the local school and church.

The number of demolitions was small prior to WWI but had become merciless by 1955, when one house was crashing to the ground every five days. Statistics reveal that since 1900, 1,200 country houses have vanished in England with a frightening proportion of them being in Yorkshire.

Idyllic Duncombe Park, overlooking the River Rye and Helmsley Castle, dodged the country house cull and is intact today but only through, some might argue, a rather fortunate sequence of events.

English banker and politician, Sir Charles Duncombe bought the 40,000-acre Helmsley estate in 1694 following the death of the second Duke of Buckingham in 1687. The Duncombes until then had been obscure Buckinghamshire squires

In 1120 the estate had been owned by Walter de L'Espec and from him, it passed through his sister to the de Ros family and again through the female line to the Manners family. During 1632 the estate passed to George Villiers, the first Duke of Buckingham who was assassinated in 1628.

A former apprentice to the London goldsmith Edward Backwell, Sir Charles Duncombe became in due course a member of the Goldsmiths' Company. Under both Charles II and James II he was Receiver of the Customs and made a fortune in banking; later in life he was said to be worth £400,000. He was elected to Parliament in 1685, and represented Hedon, Yarmouth (Isle of Wight) and Downton, supporting the Tories. Arrested in 1698 for tax fraud and imprisoned in the Tower of London he was later acquitted and knighted on October 20, 1699.

Duncombe had served as alderman for Broad Street ward in the City of London from 1683 to 1686 (from which he was discharged by Royal Commission) and for Bridge Within ward from 1700 until his death. He was Sheriff of the City in 1700, and Lord Mayor in 1708.

When Charles died in 1711 he left half of his enormous fortune to his nephew Anthony; the other half going to his sister Ursula Duncombe and in turn to her son Thomas Browne (b.1683). Changing his name to Duncombe, Thomas commissioned the building of the present house.

Duncombe Park by Colen Campbell

Work started on the house and gardens, situated immediately south-west of Helmsley, around 1713 to the designs of gentleman architect William Wakefield (died 1730) who is also attributed to additions made at Gilling Castle.

Inspiration for the building may have come from Sir John Vanbrugh (1664-1726) who had seen much of the exterior for his first major architectural work, Castle Howard, completed by 1712.

Kerry Downes in *Sir John Vanbrugh A Biography* (1987) states: '[Vanbrugh's] influence can be seen in the work of William Wakefield, notably at Duncombe Park, Yorks'.

Brief details of the house are given in the *Yorkshire Herald* February 18, 1891: 'It was a massive structure in classic style. The house contained a great hall 60ft by 40ft, and a saloon 80ft long by 24ft'.

Thomas was MP for Downton 1711-1713 and Ripon 1734-1741. He had been Sheriff, Yorkshire 1727-1728. When he died in 1746 the house passed to his son, Thomas II (?1724-1779). Thomas II was educated at Westminster and Christ Church, Oxford.

He was responsible for extending the Duncombe Park grounds to include the Rievaulx Terrace c. 1758. This took place on lands given to the Cistercians by Walter de 'L'Espec to create Rievaulx Abbey and following the Dissolution of the Monasteries in 1538 these had been purchased from the King.

Thomas II was MP for Downton; 1751-1754; Morpeth 1754-1768; Downton 1768-14 February, 1775; Downton 8 September-23 November 1779.

Thomas II died in 1779 and was succeeded by his son Charles Slingsby Duncombe (1739-1803) and then the estate passed to the latter's eldest son and heir Charles Duncombe (b.1764). Educated at Harrow, he was appointed High Sheriff of Yorkshire in 1790; sat as MP for Shaftesbury, 1790-1796; Aldborough 1796-1806; Heytesbury 1812-1816 and Newport, Isle of Wight, 1818-1826.

Although never holding ministerial office, he was raised to the peerage in 1826 as Baron Feversham of Duncombe Park in the County of York. Offices held included, Captain North Riding Yeomanry, 1794; West Riding Yeomanry, 1803; Vice President Board of Agriculture, 1816.

In 1795, he had married Lady Charlotte Legge, daughter of William Legge, 2nd Earl of Dartmouth with whom he had 12 children. Charles allegedly had an art collection that included works by Poussin,

Rubens and Leonardo da Vinci.

When he died in 1841 the barony was taken up by his eldest son, William Duncombe (b.1798). Educated at Eton and Christ Church, Oxford, he was MP (Tory) for Grimsby 1820-26, for Yorkshire 1826-31 and for the North Riding of Yorkshire 1832-41; President of the Royal Agricultural Society 1864.

Two wings, to the north and south sides of the house were built from designs by Charles Barry in 1844 and 1846. Barry was best known for his role in the rebuilding of the Palace of Westminster (also known as the Houses of Parliament) in London during the mid-19th century.

William Duncombe died in 1867 and his obituary in the *Yorkshire Post and Leeds Intelligencer* of

William Ernest Duncombe, 1st Earl of Feversham (1829-1915), known as The Lord Feversham between 1867 and 1868. Caricature by Ape published in Vanity Fair in 1878.

February 16, 1867 describes him as a consistent and energetic supporter of the Conservative cause. He had also been a strong supporter of the Ten Hours Bill. This was the Factory Act of 1847 which restricted the working hours of women and young persons (13-18) in textile mills to 10 hours per day.

During his last years he took particular pride in the improvement of the breed of Shorthorn cattle. The Duncombe Park herd took rank as one of the first herds of Shorthorns in the country. Lord Feversham was a constant exhibitor of stock at the great agricultural shows, where his animals rarely failed to carry off a prize – his principal successes were the first prize for a Shorthorn bull at the Exposition Universelle in Paris, in 1855 and a similar one at the Royal Agricultural Show at Leeds in 1861.

He was succeeded by his son also called William (b. 1829). William was MP for East Retford 1852-1857; the North Riding of Yorkshire 1859-1867. He entered the House of Lords following the death of his father and a year later was created Viscount Helmsley of Helmsley in the North Riding of the County of York and Earl of Feversham, of Ryedale in the North Riding of the County of York. Together with his wife Mabel Violet, daughter of Sir James Graham, they had seven children.

In 1877 the ceiling of the Great Hall was restored under the direction of Sir Gilbert Scott. But, on Monday January 13, 1879, the *Leeds Mercury* reported Duncombe Park had been destroyed by fire two days earlier. The fire was discovered about half-past-five in the morning. Awakened by the knocks of a chimney sweeper, three housemaids also quickly discovered that the Green Room floor and the ceiling of the Grand Saloon on fire. They instantly gave the alarm and the butler and second coachman came to the spot and stood in the room in turns, throwing water on the fire as fast as twelve servant girls could bring it in buckets. They were eventually driven out by the smoke and flames. The man who was in charge of the water pumping engine was sent for, as well as the plumber, but all the taps were frozen and it was sometime before the snow, which had fallen heavily during the night, could be swept away from the ground to find the fire-plugs.

A small hand-engine kept at the house was set to work whilst the Kirkbymoorside fire engine and brigade were summoned. But both engines were delayed.

The fire continuing to spread, it was decided to send for the steam fire-engine from York. This arrived by

The aftermath of the 1879 fire

special train about 11 am, in charge of Chief Constable Haley, Superintendent Ingram, and about 20 of the York police. They were, however, too late to be of any use, as in three or four hours after the fire was discovered the whole of the centre of the building was gutted, only the outer walls standing.

The contents of the Grand Saloon, including the valuable Library and a series of family portraits, historical pictures, and other works of art were completely destroyed. But, the two most valuable sculptures supposed to be the work of the famous sculptor Myron, which were placed in the Hall, were saved.

The contents of the Study, as well as family papers and deeds were salvaged. Three valuable pieces of tapestry were rescued from the Tapestry Room, but were damaged by being torn down. The servants' apartments and the stables formed two separate wings, one each side of the house, and these were saved by the connection being cut. These wings were filled with articles saved. Amongst them was a painting by Rubens titled 'An old woman and a boy with lighted candle'.

Lord and Lady Feversham and family were all in London at the time. Every assistance was rendered by the inhabitants of Helmsley and neighbourhood in saving what property they could. Superintendent Park and Inspector Milner, of the North Riding Constabularly, with a number of men, kept a temporary watch over the ruins and the rescued property.

As soon as the fire was known in Helmsley, the fire bell was rung at the Parish Church, just before six o'clock, waking the inhabitants who hastened to the Hall about a mile from the town. Hundreds of visitors from Thirsk, York, Malton, Kirkbymoorside, Pickering and other areas flocked to the smouldering ruins during the afternoon. Reports stated the damage was estimated at £80,000 though the house was well insured.

In Februry 1879 Earl Feversham arranged for his collection of paintings and statuary, rescued from the fire to be exhibited at the York Fine Art and Industrial Exhibition. One gallery was devoted to the Duncombe Park collection. In total around 60 works were exhibited.

The foundation stone for the new mansion at Duncombe Park was laid by the Earl of Feversham on Tuesday February 17, 1891. The *Yorkshire Herald* of February 18, 1891 gave the following information: 'The new residence will occupy exactly the same ground as that on which its ill-fated predecessor stood, the general dimensions being the same, though there will be certain modifications in the planning of the interiors. Broadly speaking the original style of architecture, English Renaissance Classic, will be reproduced...The old portico and the west wall have been preserved from the demolition of 1879, but they will form no part of the new structure. The plans have been prepared from designs by Mr William Young, of Lancaster Place, London

and the contract for the execution of the work has been entrusted to Messrs W. and J. Kirkwood of Edinburgh...The mansion will be built on freestone from the Bilsdale and Farndale quarries, both of which are on the Duncombe Park estate. The estimated cost is a little over £30,000. The Earl of Feversham invited all his tenantry to participate in the ceremonial of yesterday, and there was a large attendance of neighbouring gentry and the inhabitants of Helmsley'.

On Thursday February 8, 1894 the *Hull Daily Mail* reported that 'the north wing of Duncombe Park House, which was formerly the servants' apartments, but which soon after the great fire of 1879 was converted into a residence for himself and family by the Earl of Feversham, was early yesterday morning destroyed by fire'. The valuables destroyed included Lady Feversham's jewels, some costly tapestry, and oak cabinets.

The newspaper gave details of the rebuilding work: 'Fortunately, however, the handsome new mansion now being built on the site of the old one, and which is fast approaching completion, was not reached by the flames. The portion now destroyed was one of the two wings erected in 1846 by William Duncombe, second Baron Feversham, from designs by Sir John

Duncombe Park estate workers. [YP]

Barry. After the fire, 15 years ago the Earl had this part fitted up at great cost as a residence during the rebuilding of the house. The fire, which commenced in the chimney of Lady Feversham's bedroom, was first discovered on Tuesday night'.

Mounted messengers were immediately sent to Helmsley for the fire brigade but when they arrived, owing to the hurricane that was blowing, it was impossible to save any portion of the wing, and the brigade's efforts were directed to saving what they could of the furniture. Nothing was saved except a few of the most valuable pictures amongst which was Rubens' celebrated 'Candlelight'.

The Earl of Feversham was away from home at the time of the fire, but it was occupied by the Countess of Feversham, Lady Ulrica Duncombe, the young Duke of Leinster, and two other children of the Duchess of Leinster. On the fire breaking out the children, who were in bed, were enveloped in blankets, and with the Countess and Lady Ulrica were conveyed to the Feversham Arms at Helmsley.

William Duncombe died in January 1915, aged 85, and was succeeded in his titles by his grandson Charles, his son and heir apparent William Duncombe, Viscount Helmsley, having predeceased him.

Educated at Eton and Christ Church, Oxford, Charles was elected as MP for Thirsk and Malton in 1906 and held the seat until he inherited his title on the death of his grandfather. Lord Helmsley joined the Yorkshire Hussars, and was promoted to Lieutenant on 21 May 1902. He later commanded the regiment.

Enlisting for active service in the First World War, Feversham was killed in action on 15 September 1916 at the Battle of Flers-Courcelette, while commanding 21st Bn (Yeoman Rifles) King's Royal Rifle Corps. The battalion was formed in 1915 at Helmsley.

Charles William Slingsby 'Sim' Duncombe, 3rd Earl of Feversham was only nine when his father was killed and in time took his seat on the Conservative benches in the House of Lords.

Duncombe Park saw service as an Army hospital before being leased to the Woodard Society in May 1925 as a preparatory school for girls with fees at £150 per annum.

Charles 'Sim' Duncombe was a Lieutenant-Colonel in the 13th/18th Royal Hussars and an Honorary Colonel in the Queen's Own Yorkshire Yeomanry and fought in the Second World War, where he was awarded the Distinguished Service Order in 1945. He was Treasurer of the University of Leeds from 1959 to his death in 1963. Afterwards, the earldom and viscountcy of Helmsley became extinct while Charles was succeeded in his junior title of Baron Feversham by his fourth cousin Peter Duncombe (b.1945).

The house seemed set for a permanent institutional fate until Peter, and his second wife, Polly, summoned up immense courage in the 1980s when they decided to reclaim it to its original purpose. The girls' school lease on Duncombe Park had expired

Lady Feversham strolls around the grounds, January 1988. [YP]

and made its new home at Baldersby Park by an amicable arrangement.

An aesthete yet a practical man, Lord Feversham said: 'Financially it didn't make sense before. Then, everything seemed to come together at the right time. Also, the house was upgraded from Grade Two, with two stars, to Grade One'.

The Butler report on the economics of historic country houses in 1981 stated that institutions were not the best custodians to run houses like Duncombe and Lord Feversham agreed: 'Everyone wanted to institutionalise property after the War, but during the mid-seventies, all experts decided it was the worst possible thing and nearly always ended up in the property collapsing.'

English Heritage generously awarded Duncombe a grant which came in very useful as estimated costs for the preliminary conservation work, including re-

The Salon. [YP]

Entrance to House. [YP]

The Baroque-style house overlooks rolling countryside.
[YP]

wiring, roofing, re-plumbing and some decorating amounted to £1m.

Feversham genuinely promised that none of the cash would be squandered on what he described as the 'conspicuous consumption' evident at the turn of the 19th century. In short, he had no desire to turn the clock back and emulate the opulent lifestyle of the Victorian and Edwardian Fevershams.

For some months after moving back to Duncombe, the Fevershams had no choice but to live modestly as they had to start by 'camping out' as Lady Feverhsam described it, in the attics, while work went on in the principal rooms downstairs.

'There were moments when I would wake up in the middle of the night and think "what have we let ourselves in for," but that was before we started. Once the work was underway we felt much happier,' she revealed.

By the early 1970s the demolition of Britain's great country houses had slowed down. A reminder of what had been lost was highlighted in 1975 when the Victoria & Albert Museum staged a massive exhibition 'The Destruction of the English Country House' which also toured the provinces.

Subsequent years saw hundreds of Britain's country houses become user friendly and open two or three days a week to those eager to see the rooms which a few years earlier their ancestors had cleaned.

Duncombe has followed this trend and annually hosts spectacular outdoor events, from steam fairs to craft shows and from falcon displays to family dog shows.

The early 18th century green gardens of 35 acres (14 ha) have been described as 'the supreme masterpiece of the art of the landscape gardener'. A sundial on a decorative urn is held by the winged figure of 'Old Father Time' in Duncombe Park grounds. The sculpture is attributed to Van Nost, c. 1715.

Whilst the house closed to the public in 2011, the spectacular gardens remain open to visitors. In 2012, Duncombe Park was used in filming the period drama TV min-series *Parade's End*, and later in the second series of ITV's *Victoria*.

Peter Duncombe died in 2009 and was succeeded in the title by his eldest son Jasper but left Duncombe Park to his second son, Jake.

East Riddlesden Hall

Death duties, which posed a severe threat to the preservation of the UK's ancient homes, were commented upon by Lord Zetland (Chairman of the National Trust) at the formal transfer to the National Trust on June 1, 1934 of East Riddlesden Hall. The 17th century mansion built on a plateau overlooking the River Aire, on the outskirts of Keighley, was generously given to the Trust by two brothers, County Alderman J.J. Brigg and Alderman W.A. Brigg who lived at Kildwick Hall. The hand-over ceremony took place in front of East Riddlesden Hall. Among a representative gathering were the Mayor of Keighley (Mr E. Whalley) and members of the Corporation and chairmen and members of neighbouring authorities.

Lord Zetland said, all over the country old homes and mansions were being demolished. There were many reasons for this, but perhaps the first and foremost 'was the existence of the death duties, which were imposed with particular heaviness upon the owners of real estate, duties which compelled men [and women] to sell their ancient homes'.

The Mayor of Keighley spoke of the services the two Brigg brothers 'rendered to the district' and said they would be remembered for their generosity and public spirit.

The brothers had been interested in preserving the Hall for a number of years after quite a furore had been caused in 1913. The *Yorkshire Post* of April 9, 1913 announced the trustees of the late Colonel Bence had sold to a London firm a large part of the East Riddlesden interior fittings and furnishing in

The Brigg Brothers hand over the deeds of East Riddlesden Hall to Lord Zetland chairman of the National Trust © National Trust

East Riddlesden Hall c. 1920s, watercolour by E. Riley © National Trust

the shape of fireplaces, oak panelling, and plaster ceilings.

The newspaper revealed there was once a proposal to take down the entire building and reconstruct it in America. Details were then given of the items sold: The whole of the old oak panelling (of five rooms) and the ceilings of two of the apartments, in two different designs of elaborate ornamental work, were to be removed. The sale also included the front door and three fireplaces. The great open stone fireplace, supported by two excellently carved stone pillars was to be taken away, and along with it a smaller stone fireplace, with an inlaid over-mantel. The newspaper understood that the sale had been made.

Concern for the Hall was shared by Louis Ambler FRIBA who wrote to the Editor of the *Yorkshire Post* on May 10, 1913: 'Sir – I feel sure that all who care for ancient buildings will share my regret to learn that East Riddlesden Hall, near Keighley, is shortly to be dismantled, and that the old fireplaces, doors, oak panelling, carving and ornamental plaster ceilings have actually been sold by the trustees of the property to a London dealer, and may be scattered

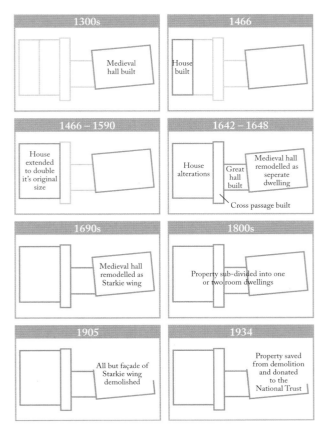

1300s	1466
Medieval hall built	House built

1466 – 1590	1642 – 1648
House extended to double it's original size	House alterations / Great hall built / Medieval hall remodelled as seperate dwelling / Cross passage built

1690s	1800s
Medieval hall remodelled as Starkie wing	Property sub-divided into one or two room dwellings

1905	1934
All but façade of Starkie wing demolished	Property saved from demolition and donated to the National Trust

Chronology of house development.
© *National Trust*

to the four corners of the earth, unless somebody steps in to prevent this act of vandalism. Surely there must be plenty of people in Yorkshire with sufficient interest in such a well-known typical example of the West Riding architecture of the 17th century to come forward with the sum of money necessary to save this historic memorial from such damage and destruction'.

At the time, William Brigg was Mayor of Keighley and, together with his twin brother John, they bought back the sold fittings for £2,000. Hoping to raise further funds from the public, the brothers were disappointed when this was not achieved.

In 1921 the Riddlesden estate was offered for sale by auction, and the lots included agricultural land, canal wharves and warehouses, cottages and gardens and the Hall itself. Although adjoining property was sold, the Hall together with outbuildings and land containing in all over 60 acres, was withdrawn at £7,350.

There were suggestions that the estate should be acquired for Keighley and in 1924 the Mayor of Keighley (Mr R. Calverley) and a number of local men who were interested in the provision of playing fields for the borough had the property offered at a figure which was not divulged.

By October, 1933, the Hall and 60 acres were sold to Harry Emmott, a Bradford builder, who was developing estates in Bradford and Bingley. After the purchase Mr Emmott said he was willing to consider offers for the preservation, on historic and antiquarian grounds, of both the Hall and estate.

Launching a rescue once again, the Brigg twins acquired the Hall and a number of acres of land from Harry Emmott, who redeveloped the remaining acreage.

Looking at the Hall's history down the centuries the *East Riddlesden Hall, Keighley, West Yorkshire. Archaeological Survey Report* (2009) states: 'Late Medieval: the manor of Riddlesden is recorded in the Domesday Book as a unit of jurisdiction, rather than necessarily as a dwelling, and it was held by a Saxon, Gospatrick, in 1086, although part of it lay in the hands of the King'.

A small medieval Hall was built on the site (becoming known as the northern section of the future complex) in the early 14th century by descendents of the Norman de Montalt family. Just a short distance south of this medieval Hall, a farmhouse was erected by the Paslew family in the mid 15th century. The latter was doubled in size between 1466-1590. From the Paslew family, the full estate passed to Robert Rishworth in 1591.

The 2,000 acre Riddlesden estate was purchased from John Rishworth in 1638 by Halifax woollen cloth merchant James Murgatroyd (b. 1575) for approx. £6,000. But John Rishworth still held rooms within the property until his death in 1664. In time, James Murgatroyd developed the medieval Hall as a separate dwelling.

The Hall in February 1954. [YP]

Alterations also included the house being developed into a two storey block; a cross passage and a Great Hall being built to join together both the house and medieval Hall.

James Murgatroyd also rebuilt or built other houses throughout the West Riding of Yorkshire. He was a Royalist (a term of abuse for the wealthier male supporters of King Charles I) and evidence of this may be seen in Royalist symbols within the East Riddlesden building.

James Murgatroyd died in 1653 and a disagreement between John Rishworth's two sons led to their family's part of the property being mortgaged to Edward Starkie. From 1672 the Starkies lived at East Riddlesden in part ownership with the Murgatroyds. During the 1690s, the medieval Hall was remodelled as the Starkie Wing and by 1708, Edmund Starkie owned the entire property. He was succeeded by his nephew Nicholas; the Starkie's male line declining by 1797.

In the 1800s the property was divided into one or two-room dwellings and ownership belonged to two men of property from Suffolk. The Hall was leased to a number of tenant farmers, chiefly from three main families, the Denbys, the Horners and the Baileys. By 1905, the entire Hall was in a poor condition, and all but the north east facing facade of the Starkie wing was demolished.

The Drawing Room. © National Trust

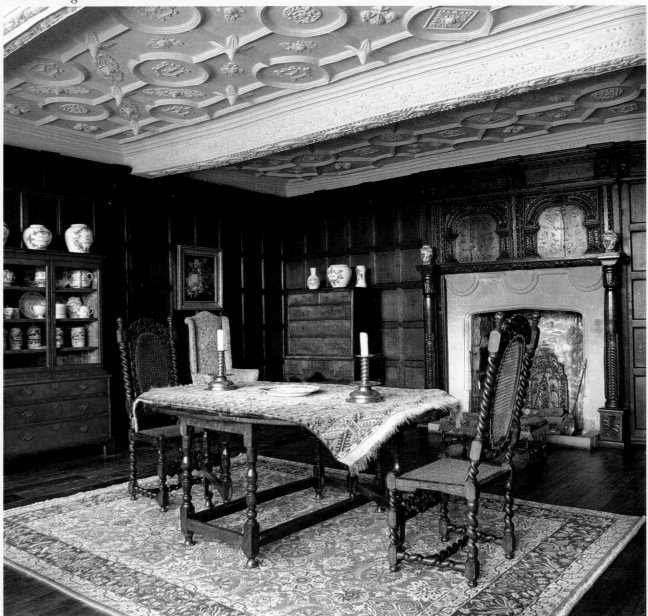

The Green Chamber. © *National Trust*

Framed in the fourposter bed is the cradle which, according to tradition, is rocked by a ghostly hand on New Year's Eve. [YP]

In 1934, the two Brigg brothers donated the Hall to the National Trust with the understanding that it would be looked after forever and the land surrounding it would be used for recreation by the local communities. The building was opened to the public on Jubilee Day May 6, 1935 at a charge of 6d (2½p).

As an exciting tourist attraction and learning centre, East Riddlesden Hall currently contains a mixed collection of 17th -19th century furniture including some locally made oak pieces; 18th and 19th century English pewter and some excellent 17th and 18th century needlework. An adjacent medieval tithe barn houses a collection of wheeled vehicles.

East Riddlesden Hall has been used as a filming location for the 1992 film Emily Brontë's *Wuthering Heights* and for the 2009 television adaptation. It was also used in 'Sharpe's Justice' episode from the Sharpe television series in 1997. The building has also featured in series eight of the paranormal television programme *Most Haunted*.

The Kitchen. © *National Trust*

Administrator David Morris Barker inspects roof timbers with a Mr Garrett during October 1983. [YP]

Fountains Hall

Sir Stephen Proctor bought the Fountains Abbey estate (founded in 1132) during 1596 for £4,500 from Sir Richard Gresham, the London merchant. Gresham had acquired the manor and dissolved monastery from Henry VIII in 1540 for £1,163. It has been speculated in extracts from J.W. Morkill's *The Parish of Malhamdale* (1933) placed on www.kirkbymalham.info, that 'Stephen derived some of his wealth from [an] early smelting undertaking which on the death of his father had evidently passed into his hands...[In1597] he was made a Justice of the Peace'. After the acquisition of Fountains lands he was involved in a series of controversial lawsuits but was knighted at the Tower in March 1604.

Proctor began building Fountains Hall between 1598 and 1610. Although re-using stone blocks – from the south east parts of the Fountains Abbey ruins – it is considered he had fresh limestone cut for the windows and main frontage. After becoming

Fountains Abbey by John Buckler © National Trust

The Frontage, 2003. [YP]

Collector of Fines on Penal Statutes to James I, Sir Stephen (baptised c. 1562) died around 1619 and the Fountains estate had passed from his heirs during the late 1620s.

Fountains Hall is an example of a late Elizabethan prodigy house. The term describes large and showy English Tudor and Jacobean houses built by courtiers and other wealthy families. Whilst Prodigy houses were constructed over the Tudor, Elizabethan and Jacobean periods they arguably have a core period from 1570 to 1620. The term was used by the architectural historian Sir John Summerson who called them 'the most daring of all English buildings'. A number were built with a view to accommodating Elizabeth I and her large entourage as she made annual tours around the country.

Stylistically, Fountains Hall perhaps reflects the Renaissance style of English architect Robert Smythson (1535-1614) who was responsible for designing Hardwick Hall, Woollaton Hall and Burton Agnes Hall. Erected close to a hillside, Fountains Hall has five -storeyed towers on the front elevation. In-between and recessed are two ranges,

also of five storeys, with the fifth storey accommodated in gables. A central block, between the gables is also recessed and contains the entrance. Of this, Pevsner in *Yorkshire the West Riding* (1959) states: 'The centre is of uncommon ingenuity and interest. It has also basement windows, then a little higher a central doorway, flanked by coupled fluted Ionic columns, then yet a little higher to the l. and r. a five-light transomed window. Above that stage a balcony railing and yet a further recession of the wall'.

Positioned on the balcony railing are five statuettes of knights. Left and right of the doorway are two more in niches, and another two more in-front of the columns of the doorway. Behind the balcony is a tall semicircular bay with two tall windows of the same height alongside. Behind the semicircular bay is the Great Chamber featuring a plaster ceiling and dramatic fireplace.

Several families have lived at the Hall, amongst them being the Messenger family c. 1627-1767 until acquired for approx. £18,000 c. 1768 by William Aislabie (1700-1781). In 1693, his father John

Fountains Hall, aerial view 2003. [YP]

Aislabie had inherited the adjacent Studley estate from his father. John was Tory MP for Ripon in 1695 and in 1718 became Chancellor of the Exchequer. He was a principal sponsor of the South Sea Company scheme and in 1720 when this financial operation collapsed, he was expelled from Parliament and disqualified for life from public office. He returned to Yorkshire and recommenced creating the elegant water garden of mirror-like ponds, statues and follies, that he had begun in 1718. By 1730 the core part of the unique garden was taking shape.

Following his death in 1742, son William purchased the Fountains estate including the remains of Fountains Abbey and Fountains Hall with the intention of extending his father's Pleasure Grounds to incorporate them into what would become England's most important 18th century water garden. Thus, the Fountains and Studley Royal estates were now united as one.

Because the Aislabie family remained at Studley Royal House, standing in the north-west corner of the lush park, Fountains Hall became redundant and was leased to various tenants. Studley Royal House had burnt down in 1716 and was rebuilt. William added a portico in 1762 to complete its Palladian appearance. A large stable block was built between 1728 and 1732.

William Aislabie was elected MP for Ripon in 1721 and sat for that area in every Parliament until his death sixty years later.

Following William's death, the estates successively passed to two heiresses in William's daughter, Mrs Elizabeth Allanson and then Mrs Elizabeth Sophie Lawrence. In the 1790s Mrs Allanson had created a 'garden feature' at the Surprise View to reveal the abbey ruins.

On the death of Mrs Lawrence the estates passed to Thomas de Grey, 2nd Earl de Grey whose nephew George Robinson, 2nd Earl of Ripon succeeded to it in 1859. George became the Viceroy of India and built St Mary's Church in the park to the designs of William Burges in the 1870s.

He was succeeded by his only son, Frederick Robinson (b.1852) 2nd Marquess of Ripon. Frederick's marriage was childless; his wife had predeceased him in 1917. He died in 1923 having collapsed on Dallowgill Moor near Studley Royal Park, after shooting 52 birds that morning.

The *Yorkshire Post* of Tuesday December 18, 1923

Fountains Hall, the Great Chamber, 1969. [YP]

announced the whole of the 2nd Marquess of Ripon's Studley Royal estate had been sold to Mr Clare Vyner (b.1894), who was second cousin of the late Lord Ripon.

Under the 2nd Marquess's will, the executors were directed to dispose of his real and personal estate. The gross estate disclosed by the will amounted to the value of £596,290, with net personality £228,970, and the duties on the property amounted to around £200,000.

The *Leeds Mercury* of June 13, 1929 noted the installation of electric lighting at Fountains Hall. The power for the lighting was supplied by a governed water turbine fixed in the old mill of the River Skell.

Fountains Hall, the Library, 1969. [YP]

On January 3, 1931, the same newspaper announced 'Fountains Hall has been undergoing extensive renovations and restorations during the last four years and the close friendship between the Duchess of York and Lady Doris Vyner has led to numerous visits being paid to Fountains Hall by the Duchess'. The *Hull Daily Mail* of Monday, May 25, 1931 gave some details of the renovations: 'The work of restoration has been carried out completely, and furnishings introduced of the period. The great part of these furnishings have been in the possession of the family of the present owner, Commander C.G. Vyner. In one of the fine old bedrooms, with its Elizabethan bedstead, the removal of a panel reveals a secret hiding place. Beneath the musicians' gallery in the banquet hall a recess contains part of a pewter service stamped with the letters 'R.V.' The initials of

Studley Royal House, ablaze 1946. [YP]

the Sir Robert Vyner who, in the reign of Charles II, was Lord Mayor of London. The gallery is lighted with electricity, but the lights take the form of old hanging lanterns. The original fireplaces are in bedrooms, parlours and halls and the banquet hall and chapel, which is above it, have each a particularly fine example. The fireplace in the chapel is thought to have come from the Abbot's house and is beautifully carved, with a representation of a biblical scene as the central panel. The central window of the chapel has, in stained glass, the arms of Sir Stephen Proctor and the various owners of the estate. The ceiling in the chapel is modern, but has been copied from a house of the same date as the hall. The balcony has been made safe and properly restored, so that visitors can for themselves see the mark of consecration in the stonework outside the chapel. The parlours, with their panelled walls, have also their appropriate furniture, and large and deep windows with their oak window seats'.

By the summer of 1931 Fountains Hall was renovated and open to visitors for the first time. A revised scale of admission charges was introduced. The entrance to Fountains Abbey and Grounds was a shilling each, and that fee was to apply to Fountains Hall but a combined ticket admitting to Abbey, Grounds, and Hall was available at 1s 6d. The Abbey and the Hall were to be open on weekdays and on Sunday afternoons during June, July and August. It was also opened the subsequent year.

In the following year, during August, the Duke and Duchess of York were pictured in the gateway of Fountains Hall whilst staying with Commander Clare Vyner and Lady Doris Vyner at Studley Royal.

During February 1939 it was announced, by the Lord Baldwin Fund for Refugees, a hostel was to open at the Fountains Hall estate. Over 30 acres of land was to be cleared. The refugees would study afforestation and all branches of farming.

A serious fire completely destroyed Studley Royal House, home of Commander Clare Vyner and Lady Doris Vyner, in April 1946. It was used as a school during the war years and until two weeks earlier by the Queen Ethelburga School of Harrogate. Valuable paintings, tapestries and furniture were saved by villagers, estate workers and police. C. Vyner and Lady Doris were staying in Ross-shire. Only the stable block survived and was later converted to a private house.

There was a Royal visitor to Fountains Hall in April 1953 when Queen Elizabeth, the Queen Mother arrived as a guest of Commander Clare Vyner and Lady Doris Vyner. During the stay the Queen Mother unveiled a memorial to two of the Vyner's children who lost their lives during the war while in the Services.

The 1960s saw the West Riding County Council acquire the entire estate of Fountains Abbey, Studley Royal parkland and Fountains Hall. In 1983 the National Trust bought the estate and then three years later, the entire area was designated a World Heritage Site by UNESCO. It gained recognition as it fulfils the criteria of being a masterpiece of human creative genius, and an outstanding example of a type of building or architectural or technological ensemble or landscape which illustrates significant stages in human history.

Fountains Hall has undergone restoration and currently offers limited accommodation in the form of holiday flats.

Harewood House

From at least 1260 a medieval manor house, known as Gawthorpe Hall, existed in the grounds of the present Harewood House. Formerly owned by the Gascoigne family, by the early 17th century Gawthorpe Hall was in the hands of Thomas Wentworth, the 1st Earl of Strafford (1593-1641). Architecturally, by this time it was a blend of medieval and classical design and the rooms included: a dining parlour; great chamber and two private rooms with a service wing containing two parlours, two pantries, a kitchen, a larder, two cellars, a brewhouse, dairy and washhouse.

After Thomas Wentworth, the house and associated lands were acquired in 1657 by Sir John Cutler. Around 1738 Henry Lascelles (1690-1753), who was the founder and senior partner of a London West India merchant house, purchased Gawthorpe

Hall and the adjoining estates of Gawthorpe and Harewood. Henry's family could trace their ancestry back to the Norman Conquest. In later years, his branch of the Lascelles family became associated with the North Riding, particularly Northallerton, holding a number of high ranking positions; Henry was MP for Northallerton 1745-1752.

Two engravings of Gawthorpe Hall - one from the north side and the other from the south - show the building surrounded by formal gardens and deer park and were produced by William van der Hagen in 1722 and 1727. They are bird's eye views, similar to those executed by the well-known partnership of Johannes Kip and Leonard Knyff, but it has been discovered Hagen's views conflict in accuracy.

After Henry Lascelles died in 1753, his son Edwin Lascelles (b.1712) took control over the family's

Gawthorpe Hall by W. Van Hagen 1721, engraver J. Harris. [Author's collection]

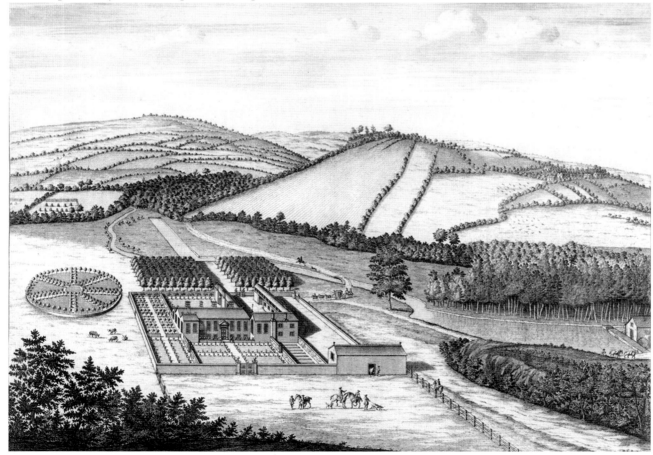

Harewood Stables. [Author's collection]

English estates and continued to live at Gawthorpe. Another son Daniel, ran the London merchant house. Born in Barbados, Edwin was educated at Cambridge followed by a Grand Tour of Europe. He was MP for Scarborough 1744, 1747; for Northallerton, 1754, 1780, 1784; for Yorkshire, 1761, 1768, 1774.

Shortly after his inheritance Edwin decided to employ Horbury-born, John Carr (1723-1807) to make some alterations to Gawthorpe. The work included a new portico for the main entrance, a garden house for the grounds and a new barn. Quite remarkably, this was only a short time before Edwin took the decision to start on a major rebuilding programme to erect a new property. It may be assumed that he wanted a house to fit his standing in politics and society, and perhaps demonstrate his vast wealth.

Building work, for the new Harewood House, which was to be financed largely from Lascelles' income from rents, started in 1755 with the Stable Block, described as an essay in Palladian design, to the west of Gawthorpe Hall. The designs were produced by John Carr and the building was erected by January 1758.

A site for the new house was chosen from early 1756 but Lascelles was undecided on the architect. Initially, Sir William Chambers, who had studied Neo-Classicism abroad between 1749-1755 was a candidate to produce designs. These were dismissed by Lascelles who nonetheless paid the designer approx. £100 for his efforts.

Visionary landscape gardener Lancelot 'Capability' Brown also produced two general plans for the house c. 1758 but details about them are sparse.

Around 1755 John Carr began to develop plans to show Lascelles. The work he had been involved with or was working on at this period included Kirkby Hall; a town house in Leeds; York Grandstand; and Arncliffe Hall in North Yorkshire.

In June, 1758 Lascelles was introduced to the

Harewood House drawn by N. Whittock, engraved by J. Rogers

A View of the Long Gallery, March 1948. [YP]

Scottish architect Robert Adam, who had just spent three years of intensive study abroad.

Once in possession of a design by John Carr for Harewood House, Lascelles asked Adam for comments. They were quite radical and he said: 'I have thrown in large semi-circular Back courts betwixt the House and Wings'.

Adam also told his family that Carr's plan did not 'admit of great many alterations' but, as his brother James put it, he 'tickled it up to dazzle the eyes of the squire'.

A compromise between the two architects' ideas was reached, as outlined by Mary Mauchline in *Harewood House* (1974): 'Carr's plan was chosen for the family apartments on the east side of the house with his circular or Octagonal Room overlooking the square inner court: Adam's for the State Apartments on the west'.

Work on the house began early in 1759 with Edwin Lascelles laying the foundation stone on March 23. In subsequent years he would keep a very keen, watchful eye on the progress of the house, workmen

and all the materials supplied. He once said to Robert Adam: 'I would not exceed the limits of expense that I have always set myself. Let us do everything properly and well, mais pas trop'.

Some of the building materials were shipped by water as far as Tadcaster and then to the building site by road, using horses to pull carriages or wagons.

Work was delayed by hard winters and, in 1762, structural problems led to the demolition of Adam's open Neo-Classical court. New work was then carried out to Carr's plan. By 1765 Robert Adam had begun designing the interior, including the ceilings, friezes and chimney pieces throughout the house.

The interior work featured the additional talents of plasterers Rose and Collins; and painters Angelica Kauffman, Antonio Zucchi and Biagio Rebecca. Adam's work often tends towards the heroic and Harewood reflects this admirably.

One of Harewood's major rooms is the Entrance Hall, where the engaged columns are reminiscent of the heavier style of classical architecture popular in the mid-eighteenth century when influenced by

Lord Burlington and William Kent.

In the Old Library, one of three libraries within Harewood House, Corinthian pilasters divide up the walls and paintings, by Biagio Rebecca, sit above the bookcases. Remaining relatively unchanged since its design by Robert Adam, the room is one that incorporates many of his typical design features, such as an elaborate ceiling, classical pilasters and a pastel colour scheme. Chippendale items include the painted blue chairs which date to circa 1771 but retain many elements of the earlier Rococo style. Biagio Rebecca has painted scenes from classical antiquity that recall the accomplishments of Roman statesmen. These may be found above the bookcases.

In the East Bedroom, which Edwin Lascelles decided would be his own, the ceiling and frieze was designed by Adam and the bed, chairs and over-mantel mirror by Thomas Chippendale. The Yellow Damask Sitting Room (later the Rose Drawing Room) is an example of Adam's penchant for a room to be 'all of a piece' where even fire-irons and door-handles were part of the overall design. Designs within the carpet echo - without copying - the pattern of the ceiling. Details running round the cornice are repeated over the doors.

Harewood House became habitable by 1771 and four years later 'Capability Brown' went to work on the park. He enlarged the lake to 32 acres, surrounding it with plantations making use of the natural features of the land in an attempt to achieve the effect of Arcadian wildness. The Pleasure Grounds were also arranged by Brown. In total, Brown spent nine years at Harewood receiving a payment of over £9,000. Thomas Chippendale, one of the most important furniture makers in Britain, produced many items of furniture for Lascelles from 1767. The cost amounted to approx. £10,000 and this was the most the furniture maker charged in his career.

The old Gawthorpe Hall was dismantled during the early 1770s, the site disappearing under 'Capability' Brown's lake.

Edwin Lascelles was first married to Elizabeth Dawes and then Lady Jane Fleming. He was made Baron Harewood, of Harewood in the County of York, on July 9, 1790 and died childless in 1795, the title becoming extinct. Brother Daniel had died in 1784 and Edwin was succeeded by his cousin

The Music Room, June 1948. [YP]

Edward Lascelles (1740-1820) who became 1st Earl of Harewood.

Born in Barbados, Edward sat as Whig MP for Northallerton from 1761-1774 and from 1790 to 1796. He was raised to the peerage as Baron Harewood, of Harewood in the County of York in 1796. In 1812 he was made Viscount Lascelles and Earl of Harewood. Edward and his wife Anne had four children.

Edward, together with his son, also called Edward (c. 1767-1814), added to the house many pieces of fine and decorative arts. The older man was a patron of music and local musicians, freely financing concerts and the repair of their instruments. He commissioned artist John Hoppner to paint portraits of various members of the Lascelles family.

Edward junior was not without some artistic talent and befriended a number of noted watercolour painters including Thomas Girton, J.M.W. Turner and John Varley. He invited them to Harewood where they produced watercolours and drawings of the house and they presently form an imeasurable asset to the collection. Additionally, Edward junior was responsible for acquiring collections of Sèvres and Chinese porcelain.

Towards the end of the 18th century landscape gardener Humphry Repton was asked to make certain alterations or 'fine tune' parts of the 'Capability' Brown's Harewood work. Further plans to enlarge the house were proposed at the beginning of the 19th century and drawings were submitted by John Carr, Peter Atkinson (Carr's successor) and Humphry Repton but were never carried out.

In the first two decades of the 19th century there were several important visitors to Harewood: The Grand Duke Nicholas of Russia, later Tsar Nicholas I arrived there in 1813; Queen Charlotte and the Prince Regent visited in 1815 to see amongst other features the fine collection of porcelain.

When Edward senior died in 1820, his second son, Henry (1767-1841) who became 2nd Earl Harewood took control. He married Henrietta Sebright (d. 1840) daughter of Sir John Sebright, 6th Baronet, and together they had 11 children. Henry was MP for Yorkshire, 1796-1807; Westbury, 1807-1812; Yorkshire, 1812-1818; Northallerton, 1818-1820. He was Lord Lieutenant of the West Riding of Yorkshire, between 1819 and 1841. Princess Victoria spent a weekend at Harewood in September 1835 and when recalling her visit she said: 'Harewood is in Yorkshire. The park seems very fine;

Lord Harewood's Sitting Room 11 May 1959. [YP]

the view from the window is very pretty. We dined in the beautiful gallery with a party of nearly 300 in number'.

During the 2nd Earl's tenure of Harewood, the house externally and internally remained virtually unchanged. His eldest son, Rt Hon Edward Lascelles, Viscount Lascelles (1796-1839) died without issue. Thus, Henry's second son, also named Henry (b.1797), became 3rd Earl of Harewood. As a young man in 1814, he was commissioned as an ensign in the 1st Foot Guards and saw action in the Battle of Waterloo and was slightly wounded. He served in the Yorkshire Hussars Yeomanry in 1820, retiring from the regular army in 1831. He was MP for Northallerton from 1826 to 1831 and served as Lord Lieutenant of the West Riding of Yorkshire from 1846 to 1857.

Henry was 44 when he inherited the Harewood title and with his wife Lady Louisa Thynne, the daughter of the 2nd Marquis of Bath, they had 13 children.

With such a large family, there was an urgent need for more accommodation, a reorganisation and an updating of the house's facilities. To execute extensive redevelopment a commission fell to Sir Charles Barry, noted for his design of the Houses of Parliament. His work at Harewood included raising the height of the wings, adding a third storey to the house, and removing Adam's portico from the South Front. His work completely altered the character of the house. The massive terraces with their fountains were also added by Barry.

Henry died in February 1859, after suffering from a fractured skull and other injuries caused by a fall from his horse while following the Bramham Moor hounds. His wife passed away in 1859.

Henry Thynne Lascelles became the 4th Earl of Harewood (b.1824). He was a widower with six children on moving into Harewood House in 1857. A year later he married Diana Smyth (c.1838-1904) and they had eight children.

The 4th Earl's tenure of Harewood House was marked by improvements made to essential utilities: lighting, heating and plumbing. Gas was installed between 1862-63. In 1866, there was a fire at the house, but was extinguished before any great amount of damage was done.

He died in 1892 (his second wife died in 1910) and a section of his long obituary in the *Yorkshire Evening Post*, June 24 stated: 'Lord Harewood has always been ready to allow the public the privilege of inspecting Harewood House, with its picturesque park, and its magnificent collection of art treasures. On the occasion of the visit of the British Association to Leeds in 1890, a large and distinguished company of scientists and their friends had an excursion to Harewood, where they were received by his Lordship, who conducted the party through the house and the grounds...'

Henry Ulrich Lascelles (b.1846), became the 5th Earl Harewood, and events of note during his occupation of the house included the sale of a number of London properties, the installation of electricity, and the visit of King Edward VII.

Henry's eldest son, Henry George (b.1882) styled The Honourable Henry Lascelles before 1892 and Viscount Lascelles between 1892 and 1929 possessed a great interest in the arts and by the age of 25 was collecting important Spanish and Italian paintings. In the First World War he commanded the 3rd Battalion Grenadier Guards. During the period of hostilities Harewood became a convalescent hospital for wounded soldiers; the family moving into the east wing.

Viscount Lacelles' great uncle, the 2nd Marquess of Clanricade was also an avid collector of paintings. When he died in 1916 he left most of his fortune of approx £2.5m., Portumma Castle and a collection of Flemish and Italian paintings to the young Henry.

Henry senior died in 1929, his son Henry George, now 6th Earl of Harewood, moved from Goldsborough Hall, to Harewood in 1930 along

Harewood House after Charles Barry's alterations. [YP]

with his wife HRH Princess Mary, the only daughter of King George V and Queen Mary. They had two children and together they enthusiastically organised an extensive restoration and modernisation of the house involving some structural work. A Dressing Room for Princess Mary was created on the main floor of the house and utility improvements such as a partial re-wiring were also completed. Goldsborough Hall was eventually leased to a school and later sold.

World War II saw Harewood once again used as a military convalescent home, with the family occupying the East Wing once more. Following the cessation of hostilities the house was due for another renovation. Before a start was made the 6th Earl died in 1947. His wife was given a flat in St James' Palace by her brother, George VI although she still retained a presence at Harewood until her death in 1967.

The 7th Earl, George Henry Hubert Lascelles (b. 1923) was the eldest nephew of King George VI and first cousin of Queen Elizabeth II. He was commissioned as a second lieutenant into the Grenadier guards in 1942. A little later, he served in North Africa and Italy. Wounded and captured at Monte Corno in June 1944 he was held as a prisoner of war in Oflag IV-C (Colditz) before escaping death in March 1945 and eventually being released in May of that year.

On Saturday April 22, 1950 the *Yorkshire Post* announced Harewood House would be open to visitors each Wednesday commencing May 3, 10 am to 6pm. Admission to the house, park and gardens was 2s, 6d; park and gardens only 1s 0d. When the grounds and state rooms were opened on August Bank Holiday during the previous year there were 12,000 visitors including many American tourists.

George Lascelles had married Marion Stein a concert pianist in 1949 but this ended in divorce in 1967. He married for a second time in 1967, Patricia Tuckwell (b. 1926) an Australian violinist.

The couple opened the Bird Garden in 1970 and still thrives today, containing a superb collection of exotic species of birds, of which more than 30 are listed as vulnerable or endangered by the International Union for Conservation of Nature.

Harewood House and grounds have been transferred into a trust ownership structure managed by Harewood House Trust. Harewood won a Large Visitor Attraction of the Year award in the 2009 national Excellence in England awards. The house was used as a major set for ITV's series, *Victoria*, the

Harewood House Bird Garden, 1973 with Lady Harewood Patricia Tuckwell. [YP]

The roof under repair during 1993 with the Earl of Harewood and English Heritage Commissioner Roger Suddards looking on. [YP]

Harewood House unveiling ceremony, May 1985, with sculptress Astrid Zydower, Lord and Lady Harewood and actress Penelope Keith. [YP]

crew using much of the State Floor, Below Stairs and parts of the estate as backdrops. The series was particularly pertinent to Harewood as Victoria was great grandmother to Princess Mary Countess of Harewood. A number of personal objects in the Harewood collection belong to the Queen and include: an English school miniature of Queen Victoria replicating a Franz Xavier Winterhalter portrait; a writing set she owned; and a watercolour she painted herself.

Lord Harewood devoted much of his life to opera and served as the editor of the Opera magazine. He was president of Leeds United from 1961-2011 and president of the Football Association from 1963 to 1972. He died in 2011 and from that time his son David (b. 1950) became 8th Earl Harewood.

From the days of Edwin Lascelles, Harewood throughout its existence has continued to evolve and continues to do so today. The house, gardens and other attractions provide a wide range of experiences for families to enjoy an entertaining day out.

The Old Kitchen. [YP]

HRH Princess Royal in the Large Gallery Room, 2004. [YP]

Hellaby Hall

Country houses and estates declined rapidly during the 20th century but, defying the odds, Hellaby Hall, formerly one of South Yorkshire's prominent houses, managed to survive several scares.

Presently situated adjacent to the busy M18, Hellaby Hall was built around 1692, with a Dutch-style gable, by Ralph Fretwell. Much information or misinformation encircles the activities of Fretwell but the overview tends to be that he was strongly associated with sugar plantations in Barbados. Allegedly, he was granted an export licence by Charles II to export horses, bred on his Hellaby estate, to Barbados to work on the sugar plantations.

The 1667 hearth tax returns reveal the Fretwell family occupied three houses in the area. They included Stainton vicarage, the family home at Braithwell, which had four fireplaces and a dwelling at Hellaby with eight fireplaces. This was probably an earlier building of Tudor style which may have occupied the site of the present Hall.

Braithwell parish registers record that Fretwell's 2nd daughter Morafe was baptised on February 14, 1690 at the house of Mr. Eyre in Bramley as Hellaby Hall

was not yet finished. Fretwell died in Barbados in 1701 and left £5,000 to each of his three daughters as well as the Hellaby estate.

Nicholas Pevsner (1959) called Hellaby Hall, 'A curious and quite dramatic house of c.1700.' He also adds: 'The front is of two storeys but with a third in a large, bold, but unquestionably awkward gable...The doorway has an open segmental entablature on Tuscan pilasters'.

Fretwell's eldest daughter, Dorothy married John Pyott, and supposedly it was to her that the Hellaby estate and adjoining farmlands, eventually descended.

In time, the Hellaby estate was owned by Sir William Eden and during the early to mid-19th century a number of occupants at the Hall are noted in newspapers. These include a Mr Samuel Clarke and a Mr John Clarke.

The property came into the possession of T.E. Morrell around 1869. His obituary in the *Leeds Inteligencer* of Friday July 31, 1914 states he had resided at Hellaby for the last 40 [or more] years, being the owner of the estate. He was widely known

Before restoration, c. 1980. [YP]

Undergoing renovation, March 1990. [YP]

as an authority on agriculture and earned a reputation as a breeder of hunters and hackneys. One of his first prize-winners was sold to King Edward VII for 500 guineas. His exceptional abilities made him in constant request as a judge at various shows. For over twenty years he represented the parish of Bramley on the Rotherham Board of Guardians and on the Rotherham Rural District Council. Morrell formerly owned a famous greyhound named 'Market Day', winner of numerous trophies, and a portrait of the dog was displayed in the Hall.

T.E. Morrell left estate of the gross value of £29,785. T.E. Morrell's son, Edward Cecil Plumpton Morrell, succeeded to the Hellaby estate but in October 1922 was found dead aged 43 years in a field with a gunshot wound. At an inquest it was confirmed his death was the result of an accident. By the following year, the Hellaby estate was occupied by P. Carnelly and during June 1926, he was offering building land for sale on the main Rotherham to Maltby road. When a large advertisement was placed in the *Daily Independent* in August 1936 offering houses for sale in the Hellaby Housing Estate, a notice stated 'Any further particulars will be supplied at the Show House on the Estate of by Mr P. Carnelly'.

In more recent times when Hellaby Hall passed to Euroway Estates (North), the company had plans to convert the building and land into a sports and leisure complex but permission was refused in the early 1970s. The company then sought listed building consent to demolish the Hall in 1976 but this was also refused and Rotherham Council was ordered to buy it by the Department of the Environment after being served with a listed building purchase notice.

Thereafter the Council spent cash keeping the building watertight but it became a regular target for vandals. Consequently, the Council came under constant pressure from local conservationists to restore the building – but said they couldn't afford to do the job. In August 1980 the Hall was extensively damaged by fire though a year later it was sold to a local businessman, for £500 on condition that he went ahead with a scheme to restore it into a pub restaurant and hotel. This did not take place and at one stage extensive shoring-up work had to be carried out to make the building safe. The Hall then went to Frewvale Construction Ltd and, in the late 1980s, to the Lancashire and Yorkshire Assurance Society. It was redeveloped on their behalf by Whitley Geddes Developments as a hotel, and was opened during October 1991 in a blaze of publicity by the Stars of TV's 'Bergerac' series, John Nettles and Terence Alexander.

Disappointingly, fate continued to play a part in the Hall's history as it dramatically closed within five months with the loss of 48 jobs, the backers pulling out of the operation. Tomorrow's Leisure bought the building for approx. £1.8 million reopening it as a hotel once more in August 1995. At the time, it was said that the Hall stands incongruously next to an industrial estate but has enough breeding to ignore it. Seemingly, it has done just that and still thrives today even though further ownership changes have occurred along the way.

After renovation, c. 2000. [YP]

Kiplin Hall

Kiplin Hall's existence today is mainly the result of Bridget Talbot's connection with the place. After falling in love with Kiplin during her youth she later returned and fought to safeguard the building's heritage for future generations at a time when many houses were falling victim to their own opulence. The National Trust rejected the opportunity to save the house in the late 1950s on the grounds that Kiplin had no history. Yet, the Hall provides an insight into the lives of Jacobean government official George Calvert, who later founded the U.S. state of Maryland, and 18th century British Consul to Livorno, Christopher Crowe. Both were not of particularly noble birth, but managed to rise to their positions through determination, integrity and reliability.

The land at Kiplin was in various hands until 1619 when George Calvert bought 800 acres there. He had been born on the estate as his father had leased

Bridget Talbot, 1970

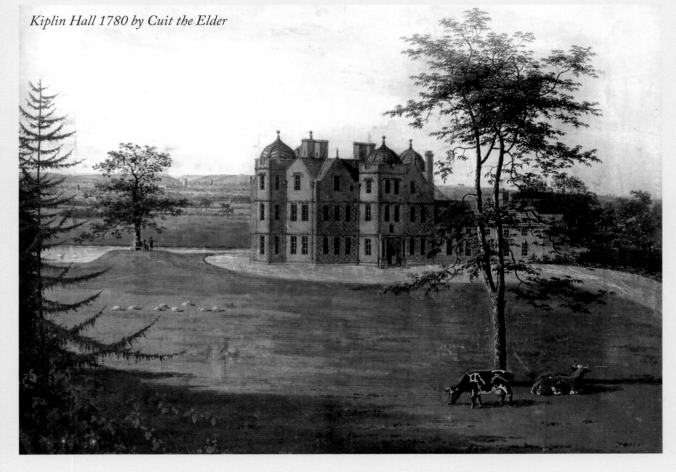

Kiplin Hall 1780 by Cuit the Elder

George Calvert

Christopher Crowe

a portion of the property in the late 1500s. Whilst a young man, he had been educated at York and Oxford, later becoming private secretary to Sir Robert Cecil, Secretary of State for King James I. Due in part to the patronage of the former and his own demeanour, Calvert was able to rise through the court hierarchy to hold some of the most important positions. He was made a knight in 1617 and was given a large estate in Ireland as a reward for his services. When he finally resigned from the service of the King, Sir George Calvert was made Baron Baltimore of County Longford, Ireland.

Before Sir George left his position, he began the task of building a grand house on his land at Kiplin. The architect is unknown but the belief is that Sir George and a contemporary at the Royal Court designed the building, which used features in fashion at the time with a few personal touches added. The exterior used red brick decorated with stone and masonry of different colours and the roofs were of lead. A rectangular shape was used for the main building and square projecting towers were added to the centre of each face of the house. Inside, on the ground floor, a Long Gallery (running east to west) split the space into two sections either side, which in turn were divided into two rooms by a main wall containing the chimney breasts. Unfortunately, little information has survived as to the original layout of the remainder of the house.

New gardens from the south-east, 1889

Kiplin's role as seat of the Calvert family appears to have diminished over successive generations and, by at least the early 1700s, Charles Calvert, third Baron Baltimore, was in residence at Woodcote Park, Surrey. After he and his son died within two months of each other, Charles Calvert inherited the lands and titles in 1715. Several years later in 1722 he sold Kiplin to his stepfather, Christopher Crowe, who resided in Italy for over ten years during his early life. As a result he had a collection of art and remodelled the house to accommodate these pieces. Other changes included the addition of a Central Staircase, the North Wing and Walled Garden. Crowe and his son – also Christopher, who inherited the house in 1749 – bought more land for the estate and by the start of the 19th century Kiplin was at the heart of 4,500 acres.

The Gothic Drawing Room, 1830

Kiplin stayed with the male line of the Crowe family until 1818 when Robert Crowe (the grandson of Christopher Crowe senior) died and the house went to his daughter Sarah Carpenter. She was married

American direct descendents of George Calvert met at Kiplin Hall 2010 to take part in the Maryland Charter celebrations. [YP]

The Library, courtesy of E. Remsberg

to John Carpenter, fourth Earl of Tyrconnel, and both lived there until their deaths, making small alterations to Kiplin during their lifetime. The estate was bequeathed to a relation of the Earl, Walter Talbot – second son of the 18th Earl of Shrewsbury – who was a career naval man, rising to become Admiral, and he was required to change his name to Carpenter in order to receive the inheritance. During his time at Kiplin, a number of changes were made, such as the addition of a gatehouse, stables and the Entrance Hall was remodelled.

After Walter Carpenter's death in 1904, Kiplin was taken over by his daughter, Sarah, who began selling off portions of the estate. In 1907 she married Christopher Turnor and moved away, leaving the

house to be occupied by tenants. By 1930 there were just 120 acres of the land owned by the family left and this process did not look like ceasing. Then, in 1937, Bridget Talbot bought Kiplin and the surrounding buildings from her cousin Sarah Turnor. Before WWI the former had been involved in a number of good causes and during the conflict she worked with wounded soldiers in Italy and refugees in England and Turkey. Afterwards, she campaigned for the preservation of her uncle's home at Ashridge House, Hertfordshire and this was successful.

From 1938, Bridget Talbot was the driving force behind the preservation of Kiplin and, had she not been completely dedicated to this task, then the Hall would almost certainly not have survived today. Attempts made to market the Hall as a place for tourists to stay did not succeed and the National Trust was unwilling to accept responsibility for the Hall's upkeep, not being deemed historically significant, even though Kiplin was granted Grade 1 listed status in 1953. When Miss Talbot died in 1971 the estate passed to the Kiplin Hall Trust which had been formed in 1968 to make sure the Hall did not suffer the same fate many others in a similar situation had experienced. Subsequently, grants were obtained from the Historic Buildings Council and from private donors to allow the first steps to be taken towards restoring the Hall to former glories.

Dress your own Skelecrow in the Walled Garden, Summer 2016

Lotherton Hall

Sir Alvary and Lady Gascoigne donated Lotherton Hall to Leeds in 1968. The donation included a magnificent garden, parkland, an art collection as well as an endowment fund. A little later the Hall became one of three art museums run by Leeds City Council, the others being Leeds City Art Gallery and Temple Newsam House.

In 1970 a costume and fashion collection was added and five years later a new gallery, with a study centre for the city's collection of early Chinese ceramics was opened. The endowment fund, augmented with government grants, has been used successfully to buy art works for display at Lotherton. Funds have been used to buy not only traditional works of art but modern pieces too. Fashion items have also been acquired. Thus, Lotherton's collection falls into three main areas: The Gascoigne family collection; objects brought from Temple Newsam House and other Leeds collections because they can be better displayed there; and works of art acquired especially for Lotherton.

Over recent years, the eight acres surrounding the house has become home to an extensive collection of endangered bird species and a herd of red deer. Housing just over 200 different species, the Bird Garden, opened in 1980 and extended in 1983, has

Opening of Lotherton Hall, 6th August 1969.
Sir Alvary Gascoigne is on the right. [YP]

developed into one of Britain's premier collections of rare and endangered birdlife.

Additionally, there is an adventure playground with equipment for all ages and mobility levels, and picnic areas and nature trails. Behind the Hall itself a further field is often used to host shows.

Lotherton Hall grew from a relatively small villa, in existence on the present site during the 18th century. This was most likely on or close to the site of an earlier house.

When Sir Thomas Gascoigne, 8th Baronet, of Parlington Hall, died in 1810 his extensive Yorkshire estates were left to Richard Philip Oliver of Castle Oliver, County Limerick. Oliver had married at Parlington, Gascoigne's step-daughter Mary Turner, in 1804. Sir Thomas's only son, Tom, had been killed in a hunting accident in October 1809. With no direct descendents, Gascoigne's bequest was on condition that Oliver assumed the name and arms of Gascoigne.

A notice in the *York Herald* of Saturday, April 2 1825 said: 'We understand that the fine mansion and estate of Lotherton, late the property and residence of John Raper, Esq have been purchased by R.O. Gascoigne, Esq of Parlington, for forty thousand pounds'.

A notice in the *Yorkshire Gazette* of Saturday April 9, 1825 gives interesting details of a sale at Lotherton Hall: 'To be SOLD by AUCTION, by Mr Chapman, on Wednesday, the 20th, and Thursday the 21st Days of April, 1825, on the premises at

Lotherton Hall with Sir Alvary Gascoigne in the Entrance Hall. 1967. [YP]

The Hall frontage April 1979. [YP]

Lotherton Hall near Aberford, (lately occupied by J. L. Raper. Esq.) the valuable HOUSEHOLD FURNITURE, and other EFFECTS; comprising Fourpost, Camp, and other Bedsteads, with Moreen, chintz, and other Hangings; Wilton and other Carpets, and Hearth Rugs; a Drawing Room suite of Rose-wood Furniture, consisting of a Sofa, two Grecian Couches, Sofa Table, two Loo and Fly Tables, Cabinet, two Easy chairs, twelve Small and two Arm chairs, with Cushions and Covers; window curtains, Cornices, and Blinds; highly-polished Steel and other Fenders, and Fire Irons; Mahogany Bookcase; Swing Looking Glasses; Mahogany and other Chairs; several Mahoghany & Painted Chests of drawers; Mahogany Dining, Card and Pembroke Tables; also, all the kitchen and Dairy Utensils; a good Swape Mangle, & c. & c.

Likewise, 10 Sheep, a Stack of Hay, all the Garden Tools and Glasses, and sundry other Articles'.

Gascoigne involved himself in agricultural matters and had a keen interest in racing. His horses 'Soothsayer' and 'Jerry' won the St Leger races in 1811 and 1824 respectively. He was High Sheriff of Yorkshire in 1816 and was instrumental in developing coal mining on his estates. He commissioned designs for remodelling Lotherton in the 1820s but no significant improvements were carried out until much later in the century.

Gascoigne's marriage to Mary produced four children, two sons and two daughters. Sadly, Mary died in 1819 and the two sons both passed away in 1842.

Gascoigne died in April 1843 and the estates were inherited by daughters Mary Isabella Oliver-Gascoigne (b. 1810) and Elizabeth Oliver-Gascoigne (b. 1812). Mary Isabella was given the name, Mary Isabella Oliver at birth. During 1811 she changed her name legally to Mary Isabella Oliver-Gascoigne by Royal Licence.

Until the two sisters married they lived together at Parlington and often spent their inheritance building schools, churches and almshouses in the area, as well as improving the working conditions of their tenants. They were responsible for building the Almshouses at Aberford in 1844 and were active in the relief of distress on the Oliver estates in Ireland during the potato famine of 1846-1847. They were also very artistic, manufacturing stained glass windows and turned woodwork to be used in their projects.

Mary Isabella married Frederick Charles Trench of Dublin in 1850 and from that time her married name became Trench-Gascoigne.

In 1851, Captain Trench's name was changed to Trench-Gascoigne by Royal Licence. He held the position of Honorary Colonel of the 2nd Yorkshire Volunteer Engineers. The couple had one son Frederick Richard Thomas Trench-Gascoigne.

Elizabeth married Frederick Charles Trench's cousin Frederick Mason Trench 2nd Baron Ashtown in February 1852. She gained the title of Baroness Ashtown in 1852.

Once both sisters were married Isabella and Elizabeth took one estate each; Isabella taking Parlington and Elizabeth, Lotherton.

Elizabeth and her husband lived mostly in Ireland, on the Trench family estates and at Castle Oliver. The marriage produced no children and when Elizabeth died at Hotel National Montreux, Switzerland in 1893, Lotherton passed to her nephew Colonel Frederick Richard Thomas Trench-Gascoigne (1851-1937) a noted soldier and traveller. She left a personal estate valued at £54,104.

Mary Isabella had died at Parlington Hall in October, 1891 followed by her husband in 1905. As well as inheriting Lotherton Colonel Gascoigne also inherited Parlington. But, he preferred Lotherton and many of the contents and small architectural features were subsequently removed from Parlington to Lotherton. Perhaps the most significant was the bas-relief marble of the classic scene 'Alcyone and Ceyx'. Parlington, the traditional Gascoigne family home, was left to become a ruin and eventually demolished during the 1950s.

Colonel Gascoigne and his wife Laura Gwendolen, daughter of Sir Douglass Strutt Galton, remodelled and improved Lotherton Hall during the 1890s employing J. Osborne Smith to produce designs. Work was also carried out to the south and west in early 20th century. By the 1930s, the hall included a new Dining Room, Entrance Hall, Drawing Room and Servants' Wing. The building work was carried out using locally sourced materials, including Castleford bricks, Huddleston lime and sand from Boston Spa.

View of the Hall taken prior to the 1903 extension

Colonel Frederick Richard Thomas Trench-Gascoigne standing with his grandson, Douglas Wilder Trench-Gascoigne killed in WWII

Laura Gascoigne, using her considerable botanical knowledge, created a series of enclosed gardens between 1903-1929. Some of her ideas took inspiration from Ellen Willmott as well as landscape gardener William Goldring (1854-1919) who worked with Laura. Information contained on the Lotherton Hall website states: 'The old Walled Garden was transformed into an "old-fashioned" garden filled with rose beds and herbaceous borders with scented flowers, tender creepers and perennials. The William and Mary Garden was built with a sunken pond and plant walls. Part of the Victorian shrubbery was made into a rock garden, with winding sunken paths and a hard tennis court was laid out overlooking the pasture. Today, the gardens are being slowly restored to their former state'.

Lotherton Hall was used as a V.A.D. hospital between 1914 and 1918 and wounded soldiers were able to use a conveniently placed Chapel restored between 1913 and 1917 during their convalescence.

The Gascoignes equipped and ran the hospital at their own expense. Laura Gwendolen Gascoigne was awarded the CBE in 1918 and invested as a Lady of Grace of the Order of St. John of Jerusalem. Two of the medical officers gave their services on a voluntary basis. They practised locally and were called Dr. Abbott, MBE and Doctor Sykes, MBE. The

Curator Natalie Raw prepares a Jacques Fath evening dress for the Age of Glamour exhibition, 2015. [YP]

Gascoignes employed two trained nurses and two V.A.D. nurses and a ward maid, while the domestic duties were undertaken by the Lotherton Hall staff. In total, approx. 655 sick and wounded soldiers received nursing care there during the war years.

Colonel Gascoigne died in 1937 and was succeeded by his son Sir Alvary Douglas Frederick Trench-Gascoigne (1893-1970). His first marriage to Sylvia Wilder in 1916 produced two children, a boy and a girl, but ended in divorce during 1935. He remarried in the same year, Lorna Priscilla Leatham. His son,

from his first marriage, Douglas Wilder Gascoigne, was killed in action during the Second World War. Although adding few improvements to the house Sir Alvary and Lady Gascoigne nonetheless enriched it with works of art acquired from their diplomatic stays abroad.

Sir Alvary was in the Diplomatic Service between 1921 and 1953 and appointed Ambassador to the USSR between 1951 and 1953. He was invested as a Knight Grand Cross, Order of the British Empire (G.B.E.) in 1953.

Lotherton Drawing Room which houses a pair of Erard pianos. [YP]

Hattie Wood views one of the exhibits at the 'Native Americans of the Plains' exhibition in Lotherton Hall, 2011. [YP]

Markenfield Hall

Hall moat and bridge, June 1959. [YP]

The Courtyard, June 1959. [YP]

East Front of the Hall, June 1959. [YP]

Sir Richard Norton. [YP]

At the time of the Norman Conquest of England, Markenfield was a manor amounting to approx. 600 acres known as Merchefeld. William de Percy, who was not involved with the initial invasion, arrived in the country during 1067 and subsequently became a significant landowner in Yorkshire, holding a large number of Knight's Fees (areas of land sufficient to sustain soldiers in preparation for any conflict), including the manor at Markenfield.

The property subsequently entered the possession of the le Bret family and a Ralph le Bret is noted as giving some of the land at Markenfield to Fountains Abbey in the 12th century. Later, his descendents

would trade more land to the monks there. By the 13th century the family were using the surname de Markenfield, lasting until the 16th century when the 'de' was dropped. A William had a house on the site during the 1200s and the Great Hall from this period survives today.

William's son John inherited the estate after his father's death and made a number of alterations to the property, c. 1310. John was in a position (as Chancellor of the Exchequer for Edward II) to easily gain permission from the King to crenellate and fortify the new buildings. As completed, perhaps during the 1320s, Markenfield Hall was surrounded by a moat and arranged in a quadrangle around an open courtyard. The south side comprised the Gatehouse, which was replaced by a new structure in the 16th century, with bridge allowing access to the Hall. The eastern range was used for accommodation, whilst the western side housed horses and cattle. The north range was the main part of the complex, with the Great Hall and a Chapel. During the 15th century a small addition was made to this side in the form of a Kitchen and Service Wing.

John de Markenfield died without issue and the Hall passed to his brother Andrew in 1323. Subsequent generations were heavily involved in local affairs and continued to provide military support for the King when needed. Thomas de Markenfield, who was alive during the second half of the 15th century, was a close supporter of Richard III, but was given a

Fletcher Norton, Lord Grantley. [YP]

Royal Pardon by Henry VII. Thomas' son Ninian also served with distinction for Henry VIII at the Battle of Flodden and was knighted as a result.

After the Reformation Thomas Markenfield (1532-1592) continued to practise Catholicism. Upon returning from a pilgrimage to Jerusalem, he became heavily involved with other nobles in the north of England, such as his uncle Richard Norton and the Earls of Northumberland and Westmorland, to restore the religion to the country. Queen Elizabeth I was quick to suppress this challenge to her authority and in January 1570 the instigators and followers of the plot had their land seized and were imprisoned along with family members. Thomas was amongst a number of Catholics who fled to live in exile, but the Queen's vengeance followed them and he died destitute. Ninian, his son, had to secure his own release from prison by relinquishing the right to claim back his father's estates.

Markenfield Hall was given by the Queen to Laurence Meres for a period before passing to Sir Henry Gates, who was a government official and MP for several constituencies during his lifetime. The estate was offered as the dowry for the marriage between Gates' daughter Katherine and Charles Egerton, later knighted, and at the end of the 17th

The Chapel, 2011. [YP]

century Markenfield passed from their son to a relation John Egerton, second Earl of Bridgewater.

The estate just formed part of the group held by the Earls (later Dukes) and was leased to farmers for a time before being sold in the mid-18th century. The buyer was Fletcher Norton from Grantley, which is only a short distance away from Markenfield to the north west, and descendent of the aforementioned Richard. Norton trained as a barrister and later became Attorney General. He was also involved in politics and after serving as an MP he was elected Speaker of the House of Commons in 1770, holding

Ian Curteis, with a portrait of the 3rd Lord Grantley, 2007. [YP]

Markenfield Hall. [Tim Hardy]

the position for a decade, at which time he was made Baron Grantley of Markenfield.

The property was not in a good state of repair at the time of the purchase and repairs were made. Baron Grantley did not move into the building, preferring to remain at Grantley Hall, and Markenfield continued to be rented to farmers for the next 200 years.

At the start of the 1980s the seventh Baron Grantley, John Norton, began the project of transforming Markenfield Hall from a series of run-down farm buildings to their former splendour. Thankfully, none of the inhabitants of the Hall had considered making any significant changes to the layout of the rooms or removing any of the period features and much was still present behind layers of wallpaper and plasterboard.

The first stage of the restoration saw work carried out on the east range, but the task was sadly interrupted by the death of John Norton in 1995. His widow, Lady Deidre, continued with the project subsequently, with the help of her second husband Ian Curteis, and in the early 2000s the Chapel and Great Hall were fully restored. In the latter, a new fireplace had to be built as the original had been moved to the undercroft in the 16th century, but this was successfully achieved using stone from the same quarry.

The last stage of the project, which is yet to be carried out (at the time of writing), is for the surrounding land to be brought closer to the original use as a deer park. Then, Markenfield Hall will have fully realised the description as one of the finest medieval estates still in existence.

The Great Hall, 2011. [YP]

Middlethorpe Hall

Little is known of Middlethorpe before the start of the 18th century, but the supposition is that there was a house on the site before the Hall was erected. Evidence for this is provided in a drawing made c. 1700 by local artist Francis Place which shows a stable block out of keeping with the design of the house. Also, just before his death Sir Henry Thompson, local landowner and MP for York, had a dovecote built in the garden in 1680.

Middlethorpe was sold at the end of the 17th century to Thomas Barlow. He was born in Leeds, but his father was from Sheffield and his grandfather had been involved in the city's steel-making industry. Francis Barlow, Thomas' uncle, was particularly prominent in this area and had several business interests that amassed him a considerable fortune. He died childless in 1689 and named Thomas as his sole heir (apart from a sum set aside for a yearly disbursement to the poor tradesmen of Sheffield), making him a very rich man.

With this wealth came the ambition to move in more noble social circles. Thomas decided that the means to achieve this was to build a lavish new country house and he duly purchased the Middlethorpe estate in 1698. The architect for the project has not been recorded, but work was soon in hand and completed in 1702.

The style Middlethorpe Hall took was not much different from that being employed in the country at the time. Red brick was used in the Flemish bond manner with stone quoins and dressings surrounding the windows. The house has three storeys with three sets of windows either side of the central two and the doorway, which has subsequently seen a porch supported by Tuscan columns added, reached by a set of stone steps. Both the front (facing towards York) and the rear of the house follow this arrangement. Originally, the roof was flat and was surrounded by a balustrade, but this was altered during the 1800s to a hipped roof with centrepieces

Middlethorpe Hall and York from the south, by Francis Place

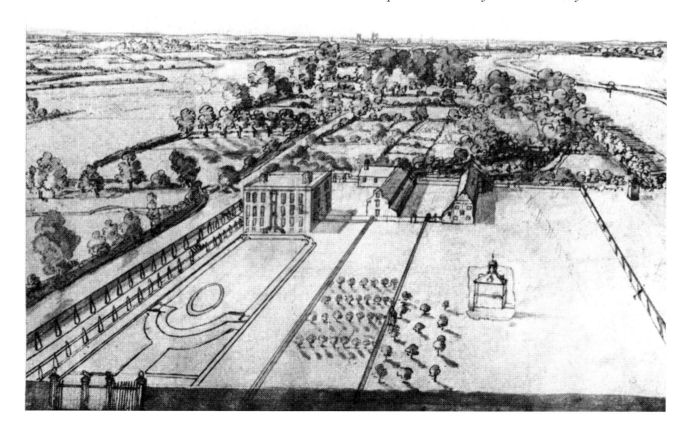

Portrait of Lady Mary Wortley Montagu (1689-1762) by Jonathan Richardson the Younger (1694-1771)

On the first floor there are three large bedrooms and a smaller one, as well as a Dressing Room. The main suites are decorated with plasterwork and marble fireplaces. The second floor conforms to a similar arrangement and ornamentation.

Thomas only enjoyed his house for ten years as in 1713 he died whilst travelling on the continent with his son, Francis. At this time the Hall was being rented to Lady Mary Wortley Montagu, daughter of Evelyn Pierrepont first Duke of Kingston-upon-Hull, and her husband.

Francis returned to the house before the middle of the decade and continued the 'country gentleman' lifestyle that his father had begun. He subsequently sold his business shares and invested in land, much of this in Yorkshire; Francis was High Sheriff of the county between 1734 and 1736.

Some of his money was also channelled into additions to the house, mainly the two wings on the east and west sides of the building, running almost flush with the southern side, but set back from the north face. On both sides the interior decoration followed the pattern set in the main house, with wooden panelling and plaster detailing. The west wing was later slightly extended to make the space suitable for use as a Ballroom.

The former Ballroom. [YP]

added to the roofline. These are topped on each side by stone eagles that once stood either side of the gateway to the Hall.

From the northern doorway a visitor would be accepted into the marble-floored Entrance Hall, which stands at an asymmetrical angle to the entry, and at the south end of this room the main staircase is separated off by a partition wall. On the left-hand side of the Entrance Hall is a reception room. Flanking either side of the staircase is the Dining Room on the eastern side and the Drawing Room on the western side. The former has fine wooden panelling with elaborately carved details and a green marble fireplace acting as a centrepiece for the room. Similar panelling can be found in the Reception Room and the Drawing Room, whilst the staircase is formed from cantilevered oak beams; the same material is used for the newels and handrail, which feature finely executed detailing.

The Staircase, 2004. [YP]

Francis died in the early 1770s and the estate passed on to his son Samuel, who was favoured over the eldest, Thomas. In 1800 John Barlow inherited Middlethorpe and during the last 13 years of his life he made several changes to the building. Upon his death, Andrew Barlow, John's brother, took over but he would prove to be the last of the male line of Barlows. In 1824 the Hall was left to John Barlow's

The Restaurant, 2004. [YP]

daughter Frances, who died childless in 1852. The estate was taken over by her second husband Dr M.E. Wilkinson and remained in this family until the early 20th century when sold.

Up to the 1970s the Hall was used as a private residence, split into flats and school. Then, an unlikely transformation was made into a nightclub called 'Brummels' and this venture was popular enough to be sustained up to 1980, when purchased by Historic House Hotels Ltd.

The south view of the Hall. [YP]

Needless to say, years of varied usage had taken their toll on the fabric of the house and a top-to-bottom restoration was necessary. Thankfully, HHH was not daunted by the project and succeeded in reviving Middlethorpe by removing the many layers of paint which vandalised the exquisite wood panelling and repairing much of the damage that had been caused to this and other features, such as the staircase, over the years. The matter of providing suitable facilities for guests was also done without disrupting the layout of the Hall and service areas, such as the kitchen, were accommodated in the basement. The stable block also proved useful in allowing visitors to be housed there after a thorough refurbishment.

HHH Ltd also owned similar properties, Bodysgallen Hall, Llandudno, and Hartwell House, Aylesbury. In 2008 an agreement was reached where all three houses became owned by the National Trust and all profits made by them are to be reinvested in the body in order to preserve and maintain these and other properties of historical interest.

Monk Fryston Hall

A settlement has existed at Monk Fryston since at least the 11th century. At some point, the land was taken into the possession of the Church and then was given in the 12th century to a group of Benedictine monks connected with the abbey at Selby. A manor house was subsequently built there as the area, which was used mainly as farmland, was rich in high-quality sandstone used in the construction of several ecclesiastical buildings in the vicinity. This required a person to be employed overseeing the quarry and they resided in the house.

The Dissolution of the Monasteries saw the land sold off and after the English Civil War the manor and house were in the hands of David Hemsworth. The family had a long history and held a number of similar properties in Yorkshire before arriving at Monk Fryston in 1680. The recorded family tree starts with Thorgil Sprakling, who arrived in England early in the 11th century as part of a Danish army and subsequently settled at Hemsworth, West Yorkshire. Swillington and Garforth were later seats of the Hemsworths.

Two generations passed before alterations and repairs were deemed to be necessary. These were performed c. 1740 under the supervision of David Hemsworth (1710-1788) and saw a large portion of the complex demolished, but thankfully the south-east corner was left standing, this dating from the 14th century. One of the main features of this section was the mullioned window with chamfered edges. Renovations were sympathetic to the overall style of the dwelling.

The walls, extending two stories in height, are of local

View from the garden, October 1964. [YP]

The South Front with vintage motor vehicle. [YP]

The Ballroom. [YP]

The Oak Bar. [YP]

sandstone with slate roof and the footprint of the building follows a horizontal 'L' shape, with the longest side facing south. A large projecting gable end is present at the intersection of the two sides with a bay window on each floor. The South Front also has two smaller gabled sections standing out from the main body of the house, with drip moulds over the mullioned windows.

Benjamin Hemsworth (1848-1923) was the last of the male line to own the Hall. In the late 19th century he and his wife, Mary, embarked upon work to alter the interior of the house and changes were made to the garden. Sir Ernest George (1839-1922) was engaged to carry out this project, which saw a Billiard and Ballroom established. The latter was panelled, had a large stone fireplace and exposed oak beams. Sir Ernest travelled extensively through Europe, also being an amateur artist, and took his inspiration from there for features in the Garden. The most apparent similarity is noticeable between the bridge and that at Lucerne, Switzerland. Mary Hemsworth was heavily involved in the decoration of this with scenes from the poem 'The Rime of the Ancient Mariner', by Samuel Taylor Coleridge.

An unusual feature of the garden at the turn of the century was a zoo. Contained therein was a number of exotic animals such as monkeys, wallabies and mongooses. There was also an aviary, housing several species of exotic birds like a golden eagle, macaw and Chinese pheasants. Both house and gardens were opened to the public a small number of times during the early 20th century.

Following the death of Benjamin, the zoo was closed and the animals dispersed. His wife Mary continued to occupy the house until her own death just after the start of the WWII. The manor was then left to a cousin, but he did not survive the conflict and afterwards the Hall and lands, which stretched to just under 70 acres, were sent to auction. The buyer was a private individual, who had held the deeds for under ten years (during which time the property was Grade II Listed) when selling to the 10th Duke of Rutland (1919-1999) in 1954.

Monk Fryston Hall subsequently changed uses from a private family residence to a hotel and the transformation was sensitive to the decor of the Hall. At the time there was an emphasis on attracting not only overnight visitors, but also customers for the restaurant and groups for functions. In the late 1960s the Hall was extended along the south-west end of the building to increase the catering facilities and the number of bedrooms available; this cost approx. £70,000.

The Duke of Rutland – and his successor – held Monk Fryston Hall until the early 21st century and since that time the property has changed hands again. Recently being refurbished, the Hall continues the traditions begun over 60 years ago.

Newby Hall

A house has been located at Newby since the 1200s, when the estate was in the possession of the 'Nubie' family. Sir Jordan Crosland (1618-1670, knighted 1642), who was a soldier for the King during the Civil War – holding Helmsley Castle from Sir Thomas Fairfax for three months before surrendering – later acquired the property and held positions as Constable of Scarborough Castle, as well as being MP for the town from 1661 to 1670.

After Crosland's death his heir sold Newby to Sir Edward Blackett (1649-1718). He was the son of a Newcastle merchant – William Blackett (1621-1680) – who had earned a fortune dealing in textiles and subsequently invested in other areas, such as coal mining, further swelling the family's coffers. William's wealth lead him into local politics and later saw him created a Baronet in 1673.

With the death of his father, Sir Edward inherited much of the fortune and sought to further cement his position in society with the acquisition of Newby c. 1685. There was already a manor house extant on the site close to the River Ure, but this was not to Sir Edward's taste and he engaged no less a personage than Sir Christopher Wren to design a new house to the north of the original. This was quite a coup, given the latter's position as Head of the King's Works, which at the time comprised the reconstruction of Kensington Palace, additions to Hampton Court and the ongoing work with St Paul's Cathedral.

Newby Hall was completed c. 1700, using bricks with quoins and drip moulds; originally there was a hipped roof with a cupola. The entrance was on the West Front and was decorated with double columns and porch.

Sir Edward was made MP for Ripon in 1689, after previously being Sheriff of Northumberland, but only held this position for a year as he did the seat

Newby in the early 18th century

The Sculpture Gallery, 1968. Picture courtesy of Newby Hall

Edward, sold his interest to Richard Elcock, later using the surname Weddell, for nearly £10,000, having been bequeathed a large sum from a relation. The money was also able to buy his son William an education in London and at Cambridge, before studying law at Gray's Inn. In the mid-1760s he went on a Grand Tour and amassed a large number of sculptures. Upon returning to England he had inherited Newby following his father's death and set about providing two wings for the house, one being necessary to house his new collection.

Architect John Carr was engaged to design the additions and to make changes to the interior and exterior of the main house, by moving the entrance from the West to the East Front. However, Weddell turned to Robert Adam to complete the interior of the Sculpture Gallery and other rooms as he found Carr's plans out of keeping with his own vision.

The Sculpture Gallery's design was influenced by Roman architecture to complement the collection and consisted of three rooms; one at each end and a central rotunda with dome – extensive use was made of decorative plasterwork throughout. Perhaps the most famous piece, which was placed in an alcove in the rotunda, was the Barberini 'Venus'. This was a

for Northumberland in 1698. In the meantime, and after the latter appointment, he returned to local judicial matters and was involved in these until his death in 1718, whereupon he was laid to rest in Ripon Cathedral.

Newby Hall remained with the Blackett family until 1748 when Sir Edward Blackett, fourth Baronet, who had inherited the estate from his uncle, also Sir

The Tapestry Room. Picture courtesy of Newby Hall

Roman copy of the 'Aphrodite of Cnidus' made in Greece during the fourth century BC and Weddell was rumoured to have paid a very large amount of money for the statue. Unhappily, the piece was sold in 2002 (commanding the highest price paid for an ancient sculpture at the time) to raise funds for restoration of the stables and replaced with a copy.

Shortly after this work was completed, architect William Belwood of York was engaged to rebuild the roof – the balustrade and cornice were installed at this time – and to add a stable block and entrance lodges.

With the house becoming a great status symbol, Weddell sought to match this personally by entering politics, returning as MP for Kingston-upon-Hull between 1766 and 1774, then Malton from 1775 to 1792. He died in the latter year without an heir and the estate was left to his cousin Thomas Philip Robinson, sharing an ancestor in Sir William Robinson, 1603-1658. Thomas was only 11 at the time of the inheritance, but he was already the third Baron Grantham after his father's death in 1786 and, also in 1792, became sixth Baronet Robinson of Newby, again taking the title upon the death of his cousin Sir Norton Robinson.

Lord Grantham spent some time at Newby and made some changes to the layout of rooms. The

The Library, 1968. Picture courtesy of Newby Hall

Adam Dining Room, located at the southern end of the house, was turned into a Library, thankfully keeping the fine plasterwork by Joseph Rose. Lord Grantham was an amateur architect and contributed the plans for the new Dining Room which was grafted on to the north face of the house c. 1810.

The daughter of Lord Grantham, Lady Mary Robinson, married Henry Vyner, who was from a family that had made a fortune from banking and related to Sir Robert Vyner, financier for the Crown

Newby Hall and Garden. Picture courtesy of Newby Hall

Major Edward Compton. [YP]

Jewels of Charles II in 1660. They were given Newby after their wedding, as Lord Grantham inherited the title Earl de Grey and the Wrest estate at Silsoe, Bedfordshire. There he indulged his architectural ambitions by designing a lavish new house in the French style.

Jane and Richard (Robin) Compton pictured at Newby Hall. [YP]

Lady Mary's most prominent addition to the estate was the Church of Christ the Consoler, which was commissioned from William Burges in memory of her son Frederick who was murdered whilst travelling in Greece. The design took inspiration from medieval English and French churches and was realised in grey stone with a white stone interior, being completed in the mid-1870s.

Robert de Grey Vyner was the next inhabitant of Newby and his mark was left in the form of the 'Victorian' wing, which extends from the north eastern side of the house, and a Billiards Room. This latter was placed above Lord Grantham's Dining Room and was decorated in the typical Victorian fashion.

Richard Compton at Newby Hall.
Picture courtesy of Newby Hall

For several centuries the various owners of Newby Hall had concentrated on making their mark with the house, whereas Major Edward Compton, who inherited the estate from his mother (Robert de Grey Vyner's daughter) in 1923, turned to the gardens and over 50 years transformed 25 acres of land surrounding the house. This work included planting borders, hedges and gardens containing a wide variety of flowers for all seasons. The centrepiece of the design was a clearing running from the southern end of the house to the river.

The love for the garden was passed on to Robin Compton in 1977 and soon after an adventure garden was provided for younger visitors, who were perhaps more appreciative of this than the Adam interior of the house, and extended the miniature railway (installed in the early 1970s) running parallel to the river.

Newby has since passed to Richard Compton and his family, allowing another generation to enjoy and contribute to the rich history of the estate.

Nostell Priory

Foundations for a small priory dedicated to St Oswald (c.604-642), the Anglo Saxon King of Northumbria, were begun by Athelward at Nostell around 1122, close to the present house. Building continued over two centuries. A story suggesting how it originally came into being is contained in the 'Nostell Act Book' a manuscript dating from the late 14th century. This claims Ralph Adlave, Chaplain to Henry I (c. 1068-1135), fell ill on a journey to Scotland and paused at Pontefract. Whilst recovering, he stumbled upon a community of hermits at Nostell. Duly impressed by their reverence, he gained royal support to establish a priory in the area. This may have sprung from a hermitage already existing and dedicated to St James.

Historians have carefully considered this claim, but submit the true story of the Priory's inception perhaps rests with Archbishop Thurston (c. 1070-1140) of York. Attempting to encourage religious life in the area, he was heavily involved in founding Augustinian houses in the north of England and the Priory of St Oswald eventually became one of the most important. Henry I gave large areas of land to the Priory; 12 pence per day from the exchequer at York; and the right to hold an annual fair on the feast day of St Oswald.

Under Prior William de Birstal, during the 13th century, the 'Nostell Act Book' records there were 26 canons and 77 servants at the Priory. Amongst the buildings associated with the premises were a Malthouse, Bakery, Brew House, Kitchen and a Carpenter's Shop. A coal mine was also a source of wealth along with well-stocked farms.

The Priory thrived until the Dissolution of the Monasteries covering the period between April 1536 and April 1540. In that time across Britain over 800 buildings – homes to over 10,000 – were lost.

Nostell's last prior Robert Ferrar, surrendered the Priory to Henry VIII in 1540. One of the King's principal agents in suppressing religious houses was jurist and diplomat, Dr Thomas Legh who was granted Nostell's buildings and land for just over £1,140.

From the time of Legh's occupation, three ranges of the old Priory buildings were transformed into a manor house, Nostell Hall. It comprised three sections including a large hall arranged around a courtyard.

General view of the house from an engraving. © National Trust

Sir Rowland Winn Fourth Baronet. © *National Trust*

elected MP for Queenborough in the short Parliament and supported the King in the Civil War. Afterwards, in 1654, a £20,000 fine was levied on him and he was declared bankrupt. Nostell was then taken by the Sir George Winn (b.1607), staying with his family for centuries.

Originally from North Wales, the Winns had financial success and a sound reputation as London textile merchants, members of the family holding such prominent positions as Draper to Queen Elizabeth I and Masters of the Merchants Guild Company. During the first half of the 17th century, the Winn's had profited from buying amongst others the lands of defeated Royalists.

George Winn was granted a baronetcy by Charles II in 1660 and when he died in 1667, Nostell passed to Sir Edmund, 2nd Bt (1644-1694) followed by Sir Rowland, 3rd Bt (1675-1722). During the latter's time at Nostell a new stable block was built.

Sir Rowland Winn, 4th Baronet, (b. c.1706) was sixteen when he inherited Nostell in 1722. During his early years, the running of the Nostell estates and others in Lincolnshire were overseen by his uncles. He was educated in Geneva then, like many other young affluent gentlemen, made a two-year Grand Tour of Europe along with his tutor, a French Protestant pastor, Jacques Serces.

When back at Nostell in 1727, and perhaps inspired by the splendid edifices seen abroad, he decided not to live in the old Hall but build a new house. This would reflect his wealth and impeccable taste. Today, the only remains of the original Priory is a building called the Monks' Refectory which has been incorporated into the Home Farm.

Funds were provided for the 4th Baronet's new house partly from his marriage to Susannah Henshaw whose father was a former Mayor of London as well as the money inherited from his own father.

Sir Rowland commissioned the Beverley gentleman architect, Colonel James Moyser (c. 1688-1751) to produce plans. These may have been executed around 1731. There is an estate map from that date in the Nostell archives which illustrates the outline of a new house resembling the one that was actually built only a few years later. One of Moyser's earlier works was Bretton Park near Wakefield, dating from 1730 for Sir William Wentworth.

Moyser knew Lord Burlington, often called 'the architect Earl', who is remembered for bringing

Legh was knighted in May 1544, and died a year later. In 1567 the estate passed to Sir Thomas Gargrave (1495-1579). Knighted in 1549, he had served as High Sheriff of Yorkshire in 1565 and 1569. Gargrave enclosed the land surrounding the Hall as a deer park and this took in farms and woodlands that previously belonged to the Priory.

Amongst Gargrave's other positions were Deputy Constable for Pontefract Castle; Steward of York Minster; Master in Chancery and Recorder for Kingston upon Hull. He was elected speaker in Queen Elizabeth's first Parliament in 1559 and became widely known for his address to Parliament of January 25, 1559 where he urged Queen Elizabeth I (1533-1603) to take a husband and marry.

William Ireland took control of Nostell in 1613, then Sir John Wolstenholme bought the estate sixteen years later for £10,000. Wolstenholme was

Palladian architecture to Britain. Moyser's original Nostell Palladian designs with the central block and four pavilions show the influence of Palladio's Villa Mocenigo at Dolo; Lord Burlington and a pupil, William Kent had also been influenced by this building in their own works.

James Paine, born in Andover during 1717, was only 19 when employed as a clerk of works to supervise the erection of the new house. Moyser perhaps did not have the knowledge or the inclination to perform the task himself. Sadly, none of Moyser's designs for the house survive.

Paine studied at the St Martin's Lane Academy and made considerable alterations to the Nostell building. Living for eight years in the nearby village of Wragby, he was also given full responsibility for the interior decoration. When completed the house would be 13 bays wide and only two of the pavilions were built (and only one survives).

Paine was also involved with work at Cusworth Hall, Stapleton, Cowick, Bramham and Sandbeck. At Nostell, he provided designs in the Rococo style for the Staircases, State Bedrooms and Dining Room. The house's main block was noted as completed by 1750; work on the interior having been started around 1747 and continued until the 1760s, the family having moved in by this time.

It is surmised the Winn family occupied the old Nostell Hall while the new house was taking shape and the former remained standing until the late 1770s.

For the grounds surrounding the house, the 4th Baronet discussed the work with Stephen Switzer (1682-1745), a gardener and writer on garden subjects, as well as local nurseryman, Joseph Perfect. However, not all the designs of these two men were fully carried out. From the mid 1750s the parkland was developed in a more naturalistic style; the upper lake was created and the public bridge linking Doncaster and Wakefield was reconstructed to a design submitted by amateur architect Sir George Savile.

Sir Rowland Winn Fifth Baronet. © *National Trust*

The Saloon. [YP]

The Pyramid Lodge. © National Trust

Before he died in 1765, the 4th Baronet was Sheriff of Yorkshire from 1731 to 1732. In 1733 he was Parliamentary candidate for Yorkshire.

Sir Rowland Winn, the 5th Baronet (b. 1739), took over Nostell on the death of his father. He was educated in Switzerland between 1756 and 1762, met the philosopher Voltaire and spent considerable sums on renting and buying horses. Whilst abroad he met and married, Sabine d'Hervart, daughter of Baron Jacques Phillipe d'Hervart, Governor of Vevey.

Inheriting the Nostell estate marked a major turning point in the house's construction as the 5th Baronet brought in Paine's main rival, the emerging Robert Adam (1728-1792) during 1766 to complete the work.

Adam, who had studied architecture in Rome in the late 1750s, rejected the Palladian style and became an exponent of Neo-Classicism which became popular from around 1750. What was the difference? To the average eye, not much. But, in Adam's case he made a decision to abandon the restrictions Palladianism imposed. Thus, his work reveals a lighter, more elegant approach.

Nostell Priory Chippendale Library Table. [YP]

Adam's contributions to Nostell began with the Library then continued to the Tapestry Room, Salon and Top Hall. Alterations were also made to Paine's rooms.

In 1777, Adam added two flights of stairs to the house's Front Entrance and produced designs for stables, a riding school and three lodges. Besides adding lodges and altering a section of the route between Doncaster and Wakefield, the 5th Baronet constructed a principal entrance to the house at

Nostell bridge on the Wakefield/Doncaster Road.
[Author's collection]

Featherstone in the form of a pyramid. Work continued at Nostell until the untimely death of Sir Rowland, killed in a carriage mishap whilst travelling to London.

The Leeds Intelligencer of Tuesday March 1, 1785 reported: 'On Sunday last died suddenly, at Retford, in Nottinghamshire, on his road to London, Sir Rowland Winn, Bart, of Nostell, in this county. He has left a disconsolate widow and two children, a son and daughter. The account of his death was received by the inhabitants of Pontefract with the most heart-felt sorrow, accompanied with a grateful remembrance of his past services in their cause, in endeavouring to restore their ancient rights and freedom of election; in which cause he spent near £20,000'.

With significant monies still owing to various craftsmen and the family's fortunes depleted, further work on the house did not continue for a number of years.

The 6th Baronet, also named Sir Rowland (b. 1775) was only 10 at the time of his father's death; the estates being overseen by Shepley Watson a local solicitor. A keen sportsman, the 6th Baronet was High Sheriff of Yorkshire in 1799, but died unmarried and without issue in 1805.

Whilst the 6th Baronet's nephew John Williamson inherited the estates and changed his name to Winn in 1805 he did not succeed to the Baronetcy. It passed out of the immediate family to a first cousin.

A major reappraisal of the layout of the park resulted in Keighley nurserymen James Hank & Co. working on an extensive planting scheme in 1808. When John died in Rome nine years later, he was succeeded by brother Charles (1795-1874), who also changed his name to Winn, and married, in 1819, Priscilla daughter of Sir William Strickland.

Entrance to Stable Yard. [Author's collection]

At Nostell during Charles' time much work was undertaken on repainting and refurnishing the house. There were even thoughts of finishing the construction work on the house with ideas supplied by York architects Watson Pritchet & Watson. Finances probably dictated this was not possible. Certainly, at one point Charles, who was an avid collector of books, paintings and furniture, even considered selling Nostell and settling in Thornton Hall, one of his houses in Lincolnshire, but sold the latter instead. Many of the precious items currently adorning the house were collected in Charles' time.

Charles and Priscilla's son, Rowland (b.1820) succeeded his father and initially lived in another family property, Appleby Hall near Scunthorpe. Discovering ironstone on his land he leased it for mining, campaigning for the Trent, Ancholme & Grimsby Railway to be built, opening in 1866. He also financed the building of houses in Frodingham and a church in Scunthorpe, the latter costing £25,000. Returning to live at Nostell from 1874, the profits from the Lincolnshire ironstone and the coal mined on Yorkshire estates encouraged him to rebuild and refurbish part of Nostell. Amongst the work carried out was the rebuilding of the north and south ranges of the stable block, the decoration and furnishing of the North East Wing, and the updating of services.

Elected MP for North Lincolnshire 1868-1885, he was Conservative Party Chief Whip between 1880-1885. He was ennobled as Baron Saint Oswald, of Nostell in 1885 when the Conservatives were returned to power. He died in 1893.

The 2nd Baron St Oswald was also called Rowland (b.1857) and before his father's death was Conservative MP for Pontefract between 1885 and 1893. In 1892 he married Mabel Susan Forbes, daughter of Sir Charles John Forbes of Newe, 4th Bt. He was JP for the West Riding and took part in the Soudan Expedition as a Captain in the

Billy the Nostell deer-keeper. [Author's collection]

Coldstream Guards. He was described as a keen golfer, sportsman and big game hunter. He died in 1919.

The 3rd Baronet, Rowland George Winn (b. 1893) was Captain in 1914 of the Reserve Officers, Coldstream Guards and was wounded in the conflict. He did not live at Nostell but the property was occupied periodically by his brother Charles.

During WWII, the house was taken over by the Royal Artillery as a training base and then transferred to the National Trust in lieu of tax in 1953. The building first opened to the public after the transfer on Easter Saturday 1954. The 3rd Baron's death occurred in 1957.

Unfortunately, in April 1980, the Breakfast Room and several adjoining rooms were damaged by a fire. Following the death of the 4th Baron St Oswald in 1984 his brother Derek became the 5th Baron.

Through the generosity of a National Heritage Memorial Fund grant of over £6m., and with the help of the family, the Chippendale furniture and other items were acquired by the National Trust in 1986.

When the 5th Baron died in 1999 his son Charles Rowland Andrew (b.1959) took the 6th Baron St Oswald title. In a further grant of £4,200,000 the National Trust acquired stable buildings and areas of the Nostell parkland in 2002. A year later the parkland was open to visitors.

The house is still the home of the present Lord and Lady St Oswald.

Lord and Lady St.Oswald pictured in the Drawing Room at Nostell Priory, with four Macmillan nurses, 1996. [YP]

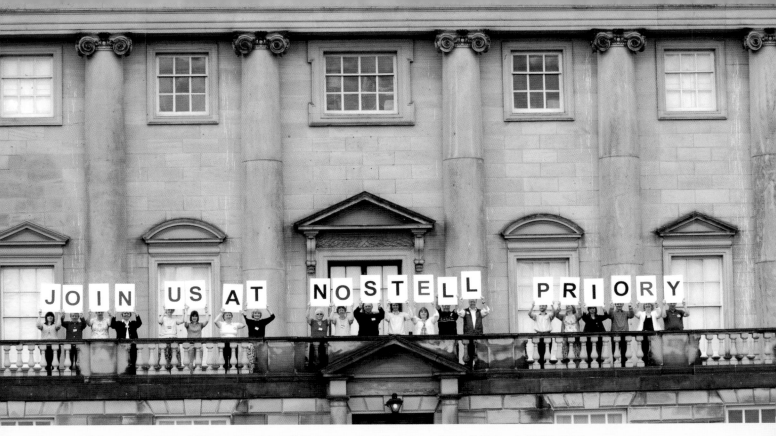

Volunteers hold up billboards at Nostell Priory, saying 'Join us at Nostell Priory', 2008. [YP]
The Tapestry Room, 2012. [YP]

Nunnington Hall

A medieval property was existing on or near the site of the present Nunnington Hall sitting on the quiet bank of the River Rye from at least 1249. It occupied land leased from the Abbey of St Mary. By the early 14th century Governor of York, Sir Walter de Teyes lived and owned land at Nunnington.

Subsequent owners of the estate included the Grene family, wealthy lawyers from Hamphsire. During the 16th century, Nunnington belonged to William Parr (1513-1571), brother of Catherine Parr, sixth wife of Henry VIII. One of the most powerful men at the court of Edward VI, William was created Earl of Essex in 1539 and Marquis of Northampton in 1547. After Edward VI's death, Parr was amongst those who attempted to put Lady Jane Grey on the throne. Convicted of high treason and sentenced to death in August 1553 after the accession of Mary I, he was released a little later and his titles were restored to him by Elizabeth I in 1559.

Whilst there is no evidence to suggest that Parr ever lived at Nunnington, the earliest parts of Nunnington Hall which are on the west side most likely date from the early period of his life.

Nunnington was Crown property during the 16th century and was both let and sub-let to a succession of tenants. One noted tenant from 1567 was Dr Robert Huicke, physician to Henry VIII, Queen Catherine Parr, Edward VI and Queen Elizabeth I, though he did not live Nunnington. Through this period of lets and sublets the Nunnington manor house was probably occupied by stewards.

A sub-lease was taken by the Norcliffe family from 1583 and over the next 60 years a number of alterations were made to the property. Thomas Norcliff extended the area currently known as the West Wing. It is also suspected that he may have added the South and East Wings though how extensive this work was remains unclear.

City Alderman and Lewisham merchant Ranald Graham acquired the freehold of the Nunnington estate for £9,500 in 1655, though Thomas Norcliff's grandson, also called Thomas, did not give up the remainder of his lease until eight years later.

Before he died in 1685, Ranald Graham rebuilt Nunnington village church, erected a charity school,

Edward Graham, 2nd Viscount Preston, and his son Charles, later 3rd Lord Preston. © National Trust

Sir Bellingham Graham, 7th Bt.; by William Beechey. © National Trust

William Rutson on grey hunter; by John Ferneley
© *National Trust*

a 'hospital' and a stone bridge over the River Wye.

His successor was his nephew, Sir Richard Graham (1648-1695), 1st Viscount Preston who plotted to return the exiled James II (1633-1701) to the throne, and was almost killed himself. Graham was MP in two periods between 1675 and 1689.

During Lord Preston's time at Nunnington, the building was extended and refronted on the South Front besides alterations being carried out to windows, and with general repairs and redecoration also undertaken. How extensive this was or if there was a noted architect involved remains unknown. Names put forward include Robert Trollope and John Etty.

Further work was probably thwarted by Preston's imprisonment in 1688 and subsequent imposed financial penalties. Individual features added during Lord Preston's time include the series of gate piers and archways leading to the walled garden on the south side of the house. Preston died at Nunnington Hall in December 1695.

He was succeeded by his son Edward who died aged 32 in 1710. Edward was followed by his nephew Charles who became 3rd Viscount Preston. Around 1720 Samuel Buck made a rough sketch at Nunnington showing not only the south facing front but a tantalising glimpse of the layout of the 17th century formal garden.

When Charles passed away in 1738, Nunnington was inherited by his two aunts Catherine and Mary. When they died, Nunnington was not occupied by its later owners for a number of years and endured a decline. During the early 19th century Sir Bellingham Reginald Graham, 7th Bt, of Norton Conyers sold the Nunnington Estate for £152,388

to wealthy Liverpool merchant, William Rutson.

Under the Rutsons, the Nunnington church was refurbished and a new school was built in the village. Rutson's eldest son John inherited family estates at Newby Wiske and Nunnington in 1867. John was an artist and collector of art and musical instruments.

Brother Henry built the Nunnington village reading room and organised an overhaul of the Hall during the late 1860s. This included the removal of the balcony on the South Front and the addition of a triangular pediment. There was also a third brother, Albert.

Margaret Rutson (born 1891), daughter of Albert Rutson, inherited both Newby Wiske and Nunnington in 1920. Described as a strong, principled character amusing and with an infectious laugh, she sold Newby Wiske and moved to Nunnington Hall with her husband Colonel Ronald D'Arcy Fife (1866-1946). She had met him at a country-house shooting party in Cheshire during 1912 and he proposed to her.

A very distinguished soldier, he was wounded in Afghanistan and served in India, Burma and South Africa (Boer War). During the 1914-1918 conflict, he won the CMG (Companion of the Order St Michael and St George) and DSO (Distinguished Service Order). He was also Mentioned in

John Rutson.
© *National Trust*

Dispatches many times. Margaret always adored Nunnington, and as a girl often stayed in a village farmhouse and became very attached to the dilapidated house.

Margaret had sold Newby Wiske to substantially modernise Nunnington and by 1917 she and her husband had adopted two young girls. The couple intended turning Nunnington into their family home, as well as bringing it back to a resemblance of its former Elizabethan splendour. York architect Walter Brierley (1862-1926) was called in for assistance. Amongst his works were civic buildings,

The West Front c. 1860. © National Trust

The South Front c. 1860 before renovation. © National Trust

The South Front after 1868. © National Trust

churches, schools and private houses amounting to over 300.

On the west side, the Stone Hall, once a Great Hall and a Kitchen was to regain its Tudor origins and be adorned with Colonel Fife's animal skins, hunting trophies and a collection of armour.

Lord Preston's former Bedchamber, complete with adjacent closet became Colonel Fife's Smoking Room. The Entrance Hall created in Lord Preston's 17th century remodelling became the The Oak Hall. Wooden panelling, originally painted, was stripped bare in the Edwardian period.

The Drawing Room. © *National Trust*

The Stone Hall. © *National Trust*

The Oak Hall. © *National Trust*

The Yorkshire Post of December 2, 1952 announced that Nunnington Hall, near Helmsley had been left to the National Trust, with part of the contents and an endowment by Mrs Ronald Fife who had died in October.

The National Trust's motto is 'Forever, for everyone' and is a charity founded in 1895 by three people who saw the importance of the nation's heritage and open spaces and wanted to preserve them for everyone to enjoy. More than 120 years later, these values are still at the heart of everything they do. The National Trust looks after special places throughout England, Wales and Northern Ireland. This includes 775 miles of coastline, over 248,000 hectares of land, over 500 historic houses, castles, ancient monuments gardens and parks and nature reserves.

Following the National Trust taking control of Nunnington Hall, Margaret Fife's daughter, Mrs Susan Clive was offered the tenancy of the property and she remained there until 1978. The estate remains in the ownership of the family. For many years now, the National Trust has spent time conserving the building whilst running it as a popular visitor attraction.

One of the most impressive permanent displays at Nunnington, and accommodated on the Attic Floor, is the Carlisle Collection of miniatures. These were gifted to the National Trust in 1970 and have been at Nunnington since 1981. They were collected from 1921 by Mrs F.M. Carlisle over a 40 year period until the collection grew to comprise a splendid display in period rooms.

The Nunnington Hall gardens sprawl over 8 acres with a main garden enclosed in a walled area to the south of the house. Completely organic since 2002, the garden combines traditional horticultural methods and modern techniques.

Of course, a house like Nunnington, which has evolved over centuries and been the home of some very interesting characters, is bound to be associated with some ghost stories. These include, amongst quite a number, doors opening and slamming shut in the dead of night, with no explanation and the sounds of weeping have been heard throughout the night.

The TV programme *Most Haunted* has visited Nunnington Hall and picked up on a few items of paranormal activity there. As a result, ghost hunts at the Hall are organised throughout the year. The Hall also holds a changing programme of contemporary art and photography exhibitions.

Oakwell Hall

Oakwell Hall, Birstall, appears much the same today, as it did when built over 400 years ago, thanks to only minor changes during its long existence. John Batt (c.1525-1607), from Halifax, built the property in 1583; the date of construction is carved in the wall above the porch doorway, along with his initials.

John's ancestors had accrued wealth over the previous two centuries and his father Henry (c. 1505-c.1572) acquired the Oakwell manor, that comprised a small farming community, during the 1560s, along with other areas of land in Heckmonwike, Heaton and Gomersal. Once settled in Oakwell, Henry and John acquired something of an unsavoury reputation having been implicated in incidents where the parish church bell was stolen and melted down; the rectory was demolished for its stones; and cash intended for building a school was diverted.

Oakwell Hall features a mixed form of construction – stone (as seen from the outside) and some timber framing techniques. Evidence suggests the Hall replaced an earlier dwelling near or on the present site as foundations from 14th and 15th centuries

have been discovered by archaeologists. Excavations have also proved the Hall and various outbuildings were surrounded by a moat.

Using contemporary architectural features, the present Oakwell Hall house stood proudly in the landscape underlining the Batt's standing as one of the area's prominent gentry.

Several surviving books give some indication of what life was like on John Batt's Oakwell estate: The Court Baron Orders 1603; The Account Book of 1609-12; and The Account Book compiled by steward John Matteson. From the first one it is indicated tenants had to abide by a code of conduct. For example, tenants were fined 3s 4d if they killed any of Batt's rabbits. The Account Book 1609-12 reveals male labourers were paid a daily rate of 7d and women 4d.

Oakwell Hall comprises a Central Hall flanked with cross wings at either end. An Entrance Porch, adjacent to the East Wing, gives access immediately to a Passage stretching through the house.

A document from the early 17th century notes that

The Great Hall. [YP]

The Great Hall showing large front window. [YP]

to the left of the passage was a Hall and also a Hall Chamber. The eventual removal of the Hall Chamber is perhaps the most significant change to the interior. The Hall's height subsequently extended to the roof with a Gallery to connect the upper rooms of both the East and West Wings. It is also noted that on the west side the ground floor contained service rooms. Originally these may have been accommodated in the East Wing as a 'New Parlour' is recorded on that side.

John Batt's sons were well educated and attended university. Robert Batt (c.1560-1617) inherited the Hall in 1607 but did not live there, leasing it to his cousins the Waterhouse family. Robert was succeeded by his son John (c.1606-1652). He, allegedly, led an adventurous and colourful life, socialising with men of similar standing to himself and even greater.

Amongst the changes to the house during the 17th century was the switch of the hearth position in the Hall. Originally a fireplace backed on to the Passage; it was moved to the Hall's north wall. The large Hall's mullioned transomed window replaced two smaller windows and a new window was inserted above the Entrance. The early 17th century may have been the period for the construction of the North West Wing in an effort to provide more service rooms. The chimney stack was added in the middle years of the 17th century.

John Batt became a Captain in Sir William Savile's regiment which took the side of the Royalists in the Civil War. After the hostilities, because of his Royalist allegiance, John was fined a tenth of his estate's value, amounting to £360.

John emigrated to America during the 1640s to seek his fortune with three of his sons. In collusion with Sir Thomas Danby of Farnley, he organised the transportation of settlers but the two men quarrelled. Two of his brothers did however settle quite successfully in Virginia.

Following John's death in 1652, his son William (c.1632-1673) took control of the family estates but decided to live at Howroyd Hall – his wife's family home. His son also called William (1659-1684) was his successor and died a strange death which has provided the Hall with a unique ghost story. This alleges, on the day he was killed in a London duel, his ghost returned home, walked through the Great Hall, past his astonished family, continued upstairs and into his bedroom. Not only did he disappear, he left a bloody footprint in the doorway.

The Oakwell estate continued to thread its way through various members of the Batt family until a break occurred in 1747 and parts of the estate were sold.

A lawyer Benjamin Fearnley bought Oakwell but his son, Fairfax, too burdened with debts, sold it during 1789. Afterwards the house was leased to a number of schools and families. Those who ran boys' and girls' schools there included Henry Millard; the Carter sisters. A notable tenant was George Maggs, a Batley solicitor.

The Passage, looking from the rear of the house to the front. [YP]

When the building housed a girls' school run by Hannah Cockhill and her daughter, they were visited by Charlotte Brontë (1816-1855) and she took inspiration from the house to include it as 'Fieldhead' in her classic novel *Shirley* – the home of her heroine.

The Leeds Mercury of April 20, 1926 reported that an organised attempt to save Oakwell Hall with its Brontë associations from being dismantled for the benefit of American or other foreign purchasers, was decided on at a conference at Birstall Council offices. A committee was appointed consisting of W. Rhodes (chairman of Birstall Council); W.O.R. Holton, and Major G.E.H. Maggs (a former occupant of the Hall for twenty years), to: Ascertain the bedrock price for the purchase of the Hall (which belonged to the Ray and Fitzroy Estates); and obtain for a reasonable period the option of purchase; and prepare a scheme for the use and administration of the Hall. Fears had been expressed that the valuable oak panelling and other rare embellishments in the Hall might be bought and taken out by antique dealers.

A decision to accept an option on the purchase for £3,000 of Oakwell Hall was made by the committee representing architectural and scientific interests in the West Riding on February 18, 1927. The sub-committee appointed to interview Messrs Newsam & Gott, agents for the owners of the Hall, the Hon. E. A Fitzroy and Mr Wheeler, reported that the owners were prepared to sell the Hall as it stood, with gardens, paddock, and moat, for £3,000

Members of the Civil War Society at Oakwell Hall for a weekend event during 2007. [YP]

including an option of purchase and giving reasonable time in which to raise the money. The owners themselves each promised to contribute £250, to any fund which was raised for that object. The meeting decided to accept the offer of the option.

In an article headed 'Oakwell Hall Becomes Public Property', the *Yorkshire Post* of January 4, 1928 reported: 'The conditions upon which Oakwell Hall, Birstall, the Elizabethan manor house of Brontë association, is to become a gift to the public from Sir H. Norman Rae and Mr J.E. Sharman, of Harrogate, were made public at a meeting yesterday of persons who had subscribed to a fund for public purchase of the Hall. Mr W. Rhodes, the chairman of Birstall

The Hall frontage, 2011. [YP]

Urban Council, presided. The meeting was held at the Hall and the two donors were present. It was announced that the Birstall Council had accepted the invitation of the donors to become public trustees of the Hall and that the contract would be signed the following day. As from today, therefore, Oakwell Hall is public property, held in trust by the Birstall Council.'

By May 1928 the donors were also financing at their own cost, the restoration of the Hall, its spacious gardens and grounds as nearly as possible to their original state. The cost was almost as much as the purchase price of the Hall (£2,500) but the task was thoroughly carried out under expert advice. The grounds were to be remodelled as an old world garden on the lines of a 16th century floral retreat.

The noted White Panelled Room was to be left in that state. Many years earlier, the oak panelling of the well-known Drawing Room was painted in a shade of pinky-white. Charlotte Brontë saw it, and liked it, for she wrote in *Shirley*: 'I cannot but secretly applaud the benevolent barbarian who had painted another and larger apartment of Fieldhead – the drawing room to wit – formerly also an oak room – of a delicately pinky white; thereby earning for himself the character of a Hun, but mightily enhancing the cheerfulness of the portion of his abode'. In other parts of the Hall, three or four windows which had been walled up were to be re-opened, and one or two rooms which had been sub-divided, were to be restored to their original dimensions.

Initially, when opened as a museum, Oakwell Hall disappointed the general public. One disenchanted visitor wrote the following in the press about the Hall: '...a scene of almost indescribable solitude and coldness...A bare stone floor, signs of decay and need for renovation, and a balcony that one could imagine might fall at any moment'.

Gradually, Oakwell Hall acquired more and more objects, appeals were launched and some significant loans were obtained from the Victoria and Albert Museum.

Displays depicted a range of periods but from the mid-1980s, following a detailed research project, the permanent displays were organised for the Hall to spectacularly reflect the Batt family home of the 1690s.

Gomersal Middle School pupils Lucy Nield (left) and Hannah Walker, both aged 13, take a close look at Kevin Walker of Dewsbury, who is dressed as a 17th century looter for a historic storytelling session. [YP]

Oulton Hall

Francis Blayds allegedly built a farmhouse on the present Oulton Hall site during the mid 18th century. This was developed a little later by John Blayds a shalloon and tammy merchant.

John Blayds died aged 75 in November 1804. He had been a Deputy Lieutenant and a JP for the West Riding, a partner in Beckett's Bank and an investor in property in both Leeds and Rothwell. He left his estate to business partner John Calverley (b. 1730) on condition the latter changed his name to Blayds which occurred in 1807.

John applied to have the common land around Oulton Hall enclosed through an Act of Parliament and was given Royal Assent in 1809. At the same time, Humphry Repton was employed to landscape the Oulton grounds for John Blayds and Armley Park for Benjamin Gott.

Considering himself as the successor to the celebrated 'Capability' Brown, Repton's proposals were presented as 'Red Books', comprising watercolour illustrations and text. Amongst Repton's illustrations for Oulton is one which shows the house as a simple farmhouse. He proposed alterations to the property but these were not accepted. Instead the house was enlarged and altered c. 1822 to the designs of Robert Smirke (1780-1867).

On February 24 1827, the *Yorkshire Gazette* reported that John Blayds, of the firm of Blayds Beckett and Co, of Leeds, had died at an advanced age.

The Oulton estate went to his eldest son also called John (born 1789), who in time reverted back to his father's original name of Calverley. He employed Sidney Smirke to make further additions to the house in 1839.

On Tuesday night August 3, 1850 there was a fire at Oulton Hall. A messenger was sent on horseback to summon the Leeds fire engines and he reached the town at 8.15 pm. The fire engines set off immediately. An engine belonging to the Sun Fire Office arrived at Oulton Hall first and the other engines a little later.

The area where the fire had started was entirely destroyed with the exception of the bare walls and so the firemen turned their attention to save the

Edmund Calverley and wife Isabella. [YP]

main building. Water was obtained from a pond in the grounds and great efforts were made to extinguish the flames. Whilst the damage was estimated to be around £1,500 the property was amply insured by the Leeds and Yorkshire Insurance office. John Blayds and his family were away in Geneva.

At the time of the fire, alterations were being made under the supervision of Leeds architects William Perkin and Elisha Backhouse (c.1810-1894) at the rear of the house, where a new Kitchen and some other rooms had just been added.

The new additions adjoined a wing at the rear and it was in the roof of this area where the fire started. Plumbers had been carrying out repairs and had a fire on the roof for melting lead. It was thought that the intense heat from this fire had caused the dry timber to ignite.

The well-furnished Library and safe where Mr Blayds kept his title deeds and articles of value were located in the part of the house destroyed but nothing was damaged. The pictures, and a great portion of the furniture were removed from the house into the grounds.

Superintendent James of the Leeds police, was present at the fire, with a number of policemen. They maintained order amongst the great crowd of people attracted to the incident from all the surrounding villages and protected the property brought into the grounds.

The Perkin & Blackhouse partnership was active between c.1838/39-1864 and involved with designing many noted buildings in and around Leeds. The firm produced designs for the reconstruction of Oulton Hall following the fire.

A drive leading south west to the Hall and additions to the grounds were created around the mid-19th century by landscape architect and artist William Andrews Nesfield (1793-1881).

John Calverley (formerly Blayds) died in 1868, his obituary in the *Yorkshire Post*, Saturday, March 7 1868, reports that for upwards of 50 years he was a magistrate and deputy lieutenant for the West Riding. 'He was not only a liberal benefactor to the poor on his estate, but invariably joined in any charitable effort and public subscription in the neighbourhood. He was an attached member of the Church of England, and in 1827 carried out his father's intentions by erecting the beautiful church at Oulton,' said the newspaper.

John Calverley's son Edmund Calverley (b. August 1826) succeeded his father. Educated at Harrow and Trinity College, Cambridge, Edmund, as a young man joined the Yeomanry, and after 13 years with the Yorkshire Hussars, retired as a captain. He became a magistrate and Deputy Lieutenant for the West Riding of Yorkshire, and patron of two livings. He employed Leeds architects Chorley & Cannon (active 1885-1903) to make additions to the Hall between 1888-1891.

Edmund's wife Isabella died in 1895 and he passed away in September 1897, the value of his personal estate being £150,288. *The Hull Packet* of September 17, 1897, reported: 'He lived almost the life of a recluse. His prime concern was the welfare of the church which his grandfather had founded for the spiritual good of its people'.

His son John Selwin Calverley (b.1855) succeeded him. John was educated at Harrow, Trinity College and was called to the Bar in 1882 by the Inner Temple. He was captain in the 4th Battalion Essex Regiment and was well known in yachting circles as the winner of numerous prizes with the yawl yacht *Brunhilde*.

He died in December, 1900 and was succeeded in the estate by his brother Captain Horace Walter Calverley (1862-1929) formerly of the 5th Dragoon Guards.

Oulton Hall became a convalescent home for wounded officers and also housed some Belgian

After years of neglect in 1987

refugees during the 1914-1918 conflict. The *Yorkshire Post* of July 30, 1918 noted the 'approaching completion of the neurasthenic hospital for officers, with 70 beds, at Oulton Hall Leeds generously placed at the disposal of the Government by Major H. Calverley, who had also consented to act as honorary assistant to the County Director'.

Under the heading 'Shell Shock Officers' Hospital at Oulton Hall' the *Yorkshire Post* of November 20, 1918 gave details about the treatment given to officers 'suffering from nerve strain'. A proportion of the 70 beds were reserved for officers transferred from various hospitals in the Northern Command; the remainder were for cases sent direct from clearing hospitals overseas. There were two sets of wards comprising ten rooms. It was stated that Oulton Hall was 'admirably adapted to the purpose of a hospital. The rooms are lofty, airy, well-lighted and well ventilated, most of them commanding a fine view of the extensive wooded park...Ample opportunities for recreation and entertainment are afforded at Oulton Hall. In the large spacious entrance hall is a grand piano and several of the patients have musical and elocutionary gifts that are at any time equal to providing an enjoyable concert; the billiard-room has a full-size table in frequent use;

The interior derelict, 1987. [YP]

Undergoing restoration, 1993. [YP]

In ruins, 1989. [YP]

the library contains hundreds of volumes; a writing room and a drawing room are large and comfortable apartments, and periodical dances are welcomed equally by officers, nurses and sisters...Many useful gifts and loans have been made to the hospital. Major Calverley is allowing the use of various articles of furniture, family portraits and other works of art'.

The Great Hall. [Courtesy Oulton Hall]

A controversial decision to close the hospital by the Ministry of Pensions, removing the soldier patients elsewhere, was taken in 1925 despite it being the only neurological hospital in Yorkshire, Lancashire, Derbyshire and Cheshire. It was revealed Oulton Hall had been economical to run – the annual rent being £2 – but patient numbers had been dwindling.

Early in 1927, the Hall was taken by the West Riding County Council and opened in April 1928 as an institution 'for the care and treatment of mental defectives'.

The obituary of Major Horace W. Calverley, who died aged 67 in September 1929, stated he had been in ill-health for several years and his condition compelled him to live abroad. Along with his wife he had taken over Down Hall, Essex from his late uncle, Lord Rockwood. Mrs Calverley had closely identified herself with affairs at Harlow and in Essex. They had one daughter Mrs Joyce Furneaux, wife of Col Ferneaux, Brockley, Northants.

The Hall and grounds were acquired by the West Yorkshire County Council in 1974 and abandoned in subsequent years until all that remained was a shell. During 1991 De Vere Hotels boldly took on an ambitious restoration programme turning the old hall into a luxury hotel. Opening on June 7 1993, the hotel was extended and upgraded six years later. Oulton Hall was taken over by AHG (Alternative Hotel Group) in 2006, and then Qhotels in 2014.

Fully refurbished as a hotel, c.2000. [YP]

Ripley Castle

Ripley Castle c.1780

For an average genealogist the unearthing of facts relating to a family over 200 or 300 years would be seen as impressive. The history of the Inglilbys goes several steps beyond this and a truly astonishing record of the family can be traced back nearly 1000 years to the time of William the Conqueror. For seven centuries the seat of the Ingilbys has been Ripley Castle near Harrogate and their relatively modest dwelling has provided suitable support to their escapades over the centuries.

At the time of the Norman conquest, Ripley (derived from the Celtic Hyrpe-Leah) consisted of two manors amounting to approx. 500 acres of farmland. This estate was in the hands of the Thweng family in the early 1300s and was used as the dowry for Edeline when she married Sir Thomas Ingleby (an alternative spelling of Ingilby) in 1308 or 1309. He was descended from Robert de Engleby, who had been amongst William of Normandy's invasion party in 1066, and later settled at Ingleby near Lincoln, living there until the 13th century when moving north to Yorkshire.

The area was a noted producer of corn and cattle when Sir Thomas Ingleby came to the estate. However, this prosperity was to be a short-lived as one misfortune after another decimated the area and the inhabitants. The Scots terrorised the area for much of the second half of the 1310s before famine broke out and the plague took anyone lucky enough to survive these calamities.

Sir Thomas does not appear to have been in permanent residence at Ripley during these times,

Sir William Ingilby, 1594–1652

battle to request quarters for the night, but he was met with a pair of pistols and a refusal for lodging at Ripley Castle. Eventually an agreement was reached and Cromwell spent the night in a chair in the Library with Jane watching over him with the loaded guns.

The bedroom on the first floor of the Tower also hosted an overnight visitor. On 16th April 1603 King James VI of Scotland rested at the castle whilst on his way to London for his coronation as King James I of England, Scotland and Ireland. An elaborate new ceiling was fitted for the occasion with the King's arms and that of the Ingilbys.

The decision was made by Sir John Ingilby to rebuild a large portion of Ripley Castle. He was the illegitimate son of Sir John Ingilby (1709–1771), who did not marry, but in spite of this was given the full benefits a legitimate heir would have expected to receive. The elder Sir John was a collector of art and acquired much on his travels throughout Europe, whilst still maintaining the estate at Ripley. Perhaps due to these absences, and the increasing age of the

Sir John Ingilby Bt. 1757–1815

but was in London as he first held a position as a lawyer, then judge. After his death in 1352 his son Thomas, who was also involved in the law, inherited the lands at Ripley. He was later knighted by Edward III after saving the King's life during a hunting trip at Knaresborough in 1357 and a market charter was also granted for Ripley.

Afterwards, successive generations of Inglebys inherited the manor and the house at Ripley. The details of the dwelling and additions made over the years appear to have been lost over the centuries, but certain facts have been passed down. In 1450 the Gatehouse (with Keeper's Lodge and Guardroom) was erected by Sir John Ingilby to ward off potentially hostile forces and in 1555 the Tower was completed by his great grandson, Sir William Ingilby. This project took several years amidst a number of alterations made to other parts of the house.

Both the Gatehouse and Tower have claim to interesting anecdotes concerning important historical figures. During the Civil War, the former was the location of a brief standoff between Jane Ingilby, sister of Sir William Ingilby (1594–1652) who fought for King Charles I at Marston Moor, and Oliver Cromwell. The leader of the Parliamentarians appeared after the aforementioned

Ripley Castle 1825, pencil Drawing by John Coney

castle, at the time of the inheritance the building was in a precarious condition and Sir John was obliged to totally rebuild the manor house.

The cost of the work was evidently over the available means of Sir John as an application to Parliament was necessary for the funds – £12,000 – to be raised through loans. He was hoping that his father-in-law would contribute some money to the project as Sir John had married MP for East Retford Sir Wharton Amcotts' daughter Elizabeth with no dowry in 1780, but this was not to be. It is believed that William Bellwood undertook the work and there was a concerted effort to preserve as much of the Tudor Tower as possible.

The old manor house was removed during 1784 and the new structure was finished in 1786, although furnishings and decorations were an ongoing process and many subsequently added reflected the character of the occupants from various periods. On the ground floor there was the Entrance Hall, Inner Hall, Round Drawing Room, Large Drawing Room, Dining Room and Morning Room. The old Tower was retained and the ground floor housed the Library, the first floor a bedroom and 'knight's chamber' on the second storey. The new building was intended to be completely independent from the Tudor Tower which could only be accessed via a door at the bottom of the spiral staircase; this also opened out onto the castle terrace. The internal doorways (and stairs) between the two buildings were only created in the 1860s.

The Entrance Hall made use of arches for the entrance ways to the staircase and Morning Room and Doric columns made to resemble marble stood at the boundary with the Inner Hall. The latter contained four alcoves and a round skylight to provide illumination. Designed in a similar manner was the Round Drawing Room at the end of the Entrance and Inner Halls. The Dining Room could be accessed from the Morning Room or through two hidden doors in the alcoves of the Inner Hall and Round Drawing Room. Both the Dining and Morning Rooms were fitted with exquisite chandeliers and marble fireplaces. A chandelier bought in Europe was hung in the Large Drawing Room and the surrounding ceiling was decorated with Italian plasterwork; similar embellishments were placed above the doorways and these were done by a local craftsman. William Peckitt of York was engaged to produce a stained glass window for the main staircase that incorporated all the coats of arms of the various branches of the family and when completed cost over £160.

With the work finished Sir John was free to concentrate on running his estate, looking after his large family and, from 1790, sit in parliament as MP for East Retford – a position which he received from his father-in-law. The relations between the two men subsequently broke down over the question of a financial settlement for the marriage between Sir John and Elizabeth. Husband and wife were forced to flee the country in 1794 due to their debts, while Sir Wharton Amcotts was returned as MP for East

Retford the following year.

The Inglebys spent their years of exile in Europe. Unhappily, the stress of the situation took a toll on the couple's relationship and by the start of the 19th century their marriage had come to an end with Elizabeth returning to England to live with a relative in her native county. Sir John had to wait until 1804 before he could set foot on English soil again as the necessary funds to pay the debts were gradually made through the sale of the estate's natural resources. Returning to Ripley Castle, Sir John lived for another ten years with his mistress Martha Webster, who bore him five children.

The manor next passed to Sir William Amcotts Ingilby, son of the above mentioned, who had also received his grandfather's fortune upon his death in 1807, subsequently making the addition to his name in recognition of this. Sir William did not occupy Ripley Castle much during his early years as he preferred to spend time in various European countries. Marriage in 1822 and positions as High Sheriff of Yorkshire and MP for Lindsey, Lincolnshire – the latter being held for nearly 10 years – managed to draw him back to the estate. Sir

William was therefore able to make alterations to the grounds and completely rebuild Ripley village, which was modelled on ones that had been visited during his European travels. The gardens at Ripley Castle had greenhouses installed during the late 1810s, then between 1843 and 1844 a lake (covering approximately 30 acres) was created.

All three of Sir William's male children died in infancy so the estate moved on to his cousin, Rev. Sir Henry Ingilby in 1854. He was the son of Sir John Ingilby's brother, also named Henry, and was 64 when he took over Ripley Castle, previously being a priest in Lincolnshire. Sir Henry lived until 1870 and passed the estate down to his son Sir Henry Day Ingilby, who remodelled the Library and provided a means of access to the bedroom in the old Tower. The next heir, Sir William Ingilby, took his role of 'lord of the manor' too seriously and managed to drive out the three pub landlords of the time and stopped people in the houses on Main Street opening their front doors after a mishap involving him and one of the occupant's children.

The next two generations of Ingilbys, Sir William and Sir Joslan, saw the financial position of the

York & Ainsty Hunt meet at Ripley Castle

family weakened through death duties and other events, but both managed to keep the estate moving forward. Sir William installed an electricity supply for the castle during 1920, whilst Sir Joslan replaced the roof. Like Sir John in the mid-1780s, this required outside financial assistance, which was provided by the Historic Buildings Council after Ripley Castle had been listed in 1953. These two events led to the public being granted access to the building for the first time during 1955.

Since this time, the role of Ripley Castle has been to remain a home for Sir Thomas Ingilby (from 1974) and his family, whilst being an attraction for visitors, several types of events, such as weddings, etc, and a filming location for television and film.

Sir Joslan Ingilby, 1907-1974. [YP]

Sir Thomas Ingilby on the roof of the old stables which were being restored. September 2002; in the background is Ripley Castle. [YP]

Members of Moscow State Circus at Ripley Castle, September 2011. [YP]
Jools Holland in concert at Ripley Castle, July 2011. [YP]

Sewerby Hall

Hull-born aviator Mrs Amy Mollinson (more familiarly known as Amy Johnson) officially opened Sewerby House and park in brilliant sunshine in front of 15,000 people on Monday, June 1, 1936. The Mayor of Bridlington said it was a pleasure to welcome the greatest airwoman in the world. Her record had not been equalled, let alone surpassed.

Councillor J. Byass then presented a key to Mrs Mollison to open the House (as it was called until the 1960s). He said he believed that in the future, people would appreciate more than now the decision of the Corporation in purchasing the estate. Many people appreciated it already, but there were others who criticised the expenditure. Before opening the door, Mrs Mollinson referred to the pleasure it gave her to visit Bridlington. She hoped that Sewerby would attract many visitors.

Earlier, in 1934, Bridlington Corporation had started negotiations for the purchase of Sewerby House, with the gardens, grounds, three lodges and more than 300 acres of land, and two farms. The sale was completed later in the year at a cost of £45,000. This marked the end of Sewerby House's occupation by a family which had stretched back centuries.

The first day's sale of Sewerby House's contents, was conducted on July 16, 1934 by Messrs Anderson & Garland of Newcastle. The day's proceedings were devoted to the sale of pictures and the auctioneer's hammer came down 250 times. Portraits, the paintings of old masters, together with views of Bridlington were keenly sought and the buyers included Colonel C. Fairfax, the Hon. Mrs Dawnay and the Countess of Chesterfield, together with buyers from London, York, Hull and Goole. The

Amy Johnson officially opens Sewerby House and Park on June 1, 1936. [Author's collection]

highest price was fetched by the bust portrait of Bishop Tunstall, by H. Van Zurch, which realised £100, while the portrait of a lady by J. Delff (1646) fetched £36, and a similar subject by G. Honthorst £50. A set of four views of Bridlington, in gilt pâpier-maché' frames, went for five guineas. The artist was unknown. The second day's sale was devoted to the furnishings of the Entrance Hall, Inner Hall, Drawing Room, Conservatory, Oak Room, Study and Bedrooms. Other items were to be offered over the course of the remaining sale days.

John Carleill, a York merchant, built a new house on the Sewerby site, shortly after acquiring the Sewerby estate in 1566. This may have been on or near the site of an earlier medieval manor house. He occupied the new house between 1566-1597. It was then held by various members of the Carleill family including: Tristram Carleill (1597-1619); Randolph Carleill (1597-1619); Robert Carleill (1659-1685); and Henry Carleill (1701-1714). In 1701 John Greame I (1664-1746), grandson of a local yeoman farmer, leased the house built by John Carleill, until buying the entire Sewerby estate in November, 1713 for £900. He had inherited his father's lands and wealth in 1708 along with a race horse, 'Champion', which won the York Gold cup in 1713.

John Greame I began constructing a new property on top of the Elizabethan house which had been pulled down. Built of brick between 1714 and 1720, the new structure was tall, slender, three storeys with seven bays. It compared with other Yorkshire properties built around the same period including Thorp Hall and Hunmanby Hall.

William Etty (c.1675-1734) has been suggested as the architect for Greame I's house. Evidence for this is based on the fact that Etty designed Sunderland Holy Trinity Church and this was for John Greame's brother-in-law, the Revd Daniel Newcombe. Etty was also Clerk of Works at Burton Agnes around 1713 and some of the decorative elements suggest York work.

Following on from John Greame I in 1746 was his third son, John II who married in 1756 Alicia Maria, third daughter of William Spencer of Cannon Hall, Barnsley. Unique and revealing details of life at Sewerby House, as well as other information, are contained in the letters she wrote over a 50 year period to family at Cannon Hall. These have survived and are contained in the Spencer-Stanhope papers held in Sheffield City Libraries.

John Greame II died in 1798 and, as he and his wife had no children, his nephew John Greame III

Sewerby Hall frontage. [YP]

inherited Sewerby. Born in 1759, John Greame III was educated at Cambridge, and married, at 23, Sarah Yarburgh of Heslington. They had two children named Yarburgh and Alicia Maria (after aunt Greame), but Sarah died in 1785. Two years later, John Greame III married Anne Elizabeth Broadley and they all lived with Aunt Greame at Sewerby. John and Anne Elizabeth's marriage produced no children. Aunt Greame remained at the house until about 1806 before moving to 43 High Street, Bridlington where she died in 1811.

By this time, John Greame III had embarked on several schemes to enlarge the property and improve the facilities. Leeds architect, Thomas Johnson (c.1762-1814) was commissioned to produce plans for both internal and external work. Two, two-storey bow-fronted wings were added on each side of the building. On completion, both the extension and the house brick work were painted to resemble stone. The West Wing was intended for the Servants' Hall, Housekeeper's Parlour and a new kitchen; the East Wing a fashionable Drawing Room.

A semi-circular portico, with Doric columns and semi-circular steps was erected as well as a new stable block about 1825. Five years later a new Dining Room was completed with another bedroom and Dressing Room above.

The parkland surrounding the House was developed in stages, and probably the most significant one occurred in 1811 when 843 acres of open arable fields were enclosed and awarded to John Greame III. This gave him the freedom to begin creating a park to complement the House.

John Greame III became JP and Deputy Lieutenant of the East Riding and died at the age of 81 in 1841; his wife shortly afterwards. John Greame's son Yarburgh Greame took over from his father, though he had become actively involved in managing the estate for some years earlier.

During Yarburgh Greame's occupation of the House a number of alterations were carried out: the wings were raised to the full height of the main house; and the central pediment and the eaves cornice were rebuilt. Work within the grounds included the construction of an Orangery; an archway, featuring Doric pilasters and a Greek key pattern on the blocking course, to the west side; an entrance gateway, from Sewerby village, with flanking lodges; and a clock tower added to the stables. Hull architect Henry Francis Lockwood was entrusted with producing designs for the work.

Further developments to the parkland were made possible by the purchase of additional property by Yarburgh Greame in 1850. Outside the estate, he

The Orchestra at Sewerby [Author's collection]

S. T. Thompson, former borough librarian and curator at Sewerby Hall, arranges the newly acquired collection of Amy Johnson memorabilia in March 1959. [YP]

provided a church at Sewerby; a school for the village; and contributed to the restoration of the Priory Church at Bridlington. He served as High Sheriff of Yorkshire in 1848.

Sewerby House's occupants at the time of the 1851 census included Yarburgh Greame and 11 servants. Greame succeeded to the Heslington estates in 1852 on the death of his uncle N.E. Yarburgh and then assumed by Royal Licence the surname of Yarburgh, becoming Yarburgh Yarburgh. Before he died a bachelor in 1856, he began an extensive restoration of Heslington Hall. His obituary of February 2, 1856 in the *Yorkshire Gazette*, mentioned: 'Possessed of ample possessions, he liberally dispensed to the wants and necessities not only of the poor on his own estates, but his charity had a much wider range. The extent of his benevolence could only be equalled by the quiet unostentatious manner in which it was dispensed'.

Yarburgh's estates passed to his sister Mrs Alicia Maria who had married George Lloyd. When she died a widow in 1867 her Heslington and Sewerby

Sewerby Hall Horse Pageant May, 1993. [YP]

The Drawing Room, August 2014

The Kitchen, August 2014

estates were split between her two sons. Heslington was inherited by eldest son George John who changed his surname to Yarburgh; Sewerby to her younger son Yarburgh Gamaliel who adopted the name of Lloyd-Greame.

Yarburgh Gamaliel Lloyd-Greame (1813-1890) was a vicar in Lincolnshire before his inheritance, relinquishing this position to move to Sewerby. For the remainder of his life he became deeply involved with numerous philanthropic causes.

He was succeeded by his son Colonel Yarburgh George Lloyd-Greame (1840-1928) who made a number of house improvements and additions. Listed amongst these were, extending the house to the rear and adding a new Dining Room; turning the old Dining Room into a Billiard Room; restoration of the conservatory; the installation of WCs and a new laundry.

Amongst the ground floor rooms at the outset of the 20th century were the Entrance Hall, Oak Room, Study, Dining Room and Library and Billiard room. On the first floor the rooms included the Blue Bedroom, Georgian Panelled Bedroom and Regency Upstairs Sitting Room. The second floor mainly contained servants' rooms.

Following Colonel Yarburgh George Lloyd-Greame's death, his eldest son Yarburgh Lloyd-Greame occupied the house until it was sold along with 411 acres to Bridlington Corporation in 1934. He then moved to Kingthorpe Hall near Pickering.

Sewerby Hall's 50 acres of mature parkland has since developed into one of the gems of the Yorkshire coastline, accommodating a number of recreational facilities. Amongst these are formal gardens, a small zoo, an adventure playground, golf and putting greens, picnic areas, besides a shop and cafe within a converted stable block.

During 2012, a substantial Heritage Lottery Fund grant along with a significant contribution from the East Riding of Yorkshire Council enabled the interior of the Hall to undergo a major restoration and refurbishment programme. This has seen the Hall interior reflect its former Edwardian appearance when it was the home of Yarburgh George Lloyd-Greame, complete with a reconstructed Servants' Wing and working kitchen. Objects have been loaned from the Victoria and Albert Museum as well as other major museums.

A performance by the Markina Sword Dance team from the Basque area of Spain. [YP]

Shibden Hall

William Otes, a textile merchant of Southowram, bought land at Shibden (then named Schepdene) in the early fifteenth century. He subsequently built a house there and this was completed by at least 1420. The building comprised the present central section of the property (from gable to gable) and short section on the eastern and western sides (kitchen and Savile room respectively).

The Main Hall (also known as the 'Housebody') was originally only one room, which was shorter and narrower than today. Upstairs, on the western side, there was the North Chamber and Red Room. The former was redecorated in the 1600s and much of the furniture in the room dates from this period. Similarly, the latter took the present layout in the 17th century, although the fireplace is 100 years older. An interesting area partitioned off in the room is the Powder Closet, where wigs where stored and powdered.

Otes' grandson, also named William, subsequently took over the Hall. He married three times, with the

The Hall from the south west

second and last marriages producing children – a girl and a boy respectively. As some time elapsed between the birth of the two children William's first will left the estate and house to his daughter Joan. After her marriage to Robert Savile, William attempted to change the document so the sole beneficiary was his son Gilbert. A lengthy legal battle followed as Savile did not want to lose his claim. The final judgment saw Gilbert take half of the income of the estate for life, whilst the Saviles retained the other half and the property.

The Hall from the south east

Anne Lister. [YP]

The Housebody

Some work was carried out to the house around this time as the Main Hall had a first floor added and a room there was used for hanging and storing meat, being designated the 'Flesh Chamber'. Subsequently, the frontage of the Main Hall was extended forward by 3 ft and a new fireplace and chimney installed. The Porch Chamber was also built at this time, but with the window accommodating a smaller area. Joan and Robert left their mark – literally – on the western room of the house, later being called the Savile Room, as their initials and family crest are mounted on to the ceiling by bosses. The wooden panelling in the room was added at a later date.

Joan and Robert's daughter Sibel was bequeathed the Hall in 1522. She married Robert Waterhouse, who was from a family of bailiffs that had been involved in collecting money for Lewes Priory. At the time of the Dissolution of the Monasteries, the Waterhouses were able to buy some of the rights to administer revenue from land at Halifax. However, three generations later the family was in dire straits and Shibden had to be sold in 1612. Before the family left the New Buttery was built behind the

Housebody, although the panelling was added sometime during the following century, and the Oak Room was situated above. The Old Buttery later became the Study and was panelled in the 1700s.

The new occupants were Mrs Crowther and her nephew John Hemingway, but both died not too long afterwards and the latter's four daughters were left the Hall under the guardianship of their uncle Samuel Lister, a local merchant. Two of the girls later married Lister's sons and the house passed down through the male line of the family until 1702 when jumping to a relative, James Lister. A dispute with the previous occupant's widow and her new husband stopped him taking possession until the end of the decade.

Anne Lister – perhaps the most famous resident of Shibden Hall – became the owner in 1836, although she had lived there and managed the affairs for a number of years previously. She was the daughter of Jeremy Lister, who is known for having a diary published which records his exploits during the

The Dining Room. [YP]

Woodkirk Secondary School, Morley pupils and teacher pictured in the reconstructed pub at Shibden during September 1973. Unfortunately for the pupils it was strictly a teetotal lesson. [YP]

Bedroom at Shibden.

American War of Independence. Like her father, Anne kept a record of her life, which included a lot of travelling around Europe beside the day to day running of the Hall and overseeing the modifications being made. The journals also contain an interesting insight into Anne's life as a lesbian and this aspect has formed the basis for a BBC documentary and drama.

Anne made the greatest impact to the Hall by building the tower (west side), which has a room on the ground floor, a landing at first floor level and chamber at the top. In the Main Hall, new panelling was added, as well as a new staircase. Samuel Gray was engaged to make changes to the garden and two terraces were laid out, along with the lake.

After Anne Lister died in 1840, whilst travelling in Eastern Europe, Dr John Lister moved into the Hall. His main contribution to the history of the building was extending and remodelling the dining room c. 1855. At this time an interesting discovery was made behind the wooden panels, namely Elizabethan-era wall paintings.

Dr Lister's son, also John, was the last of the family to hold Shibden. In 1923 he sold the property to Mr A.S. McCrea, but was allowed to say a resident until his death, which occurred in 1933. At this time the Hall was gifted to Halifax Corporation, while just under 100 acres of surrounding land had been taken over in 1926 and became Shibden Park. The Hall was subsequently opened as a museum, celebrating the building's several centuries in existence, the architectural heritage and the lives of the people who lived there.

Councillor and Community Services cabinet member Lorraine Stott is dressed as Ann Lister during a press announcement. She is pictured with Shibden Hall employees Deborah Comwin-Platt who is pictured as a maid and Jeffrey Andrews as a footman. [YP]

Sledmere House

At Sledmere House around noon on Tuesday May 23, 1911, the owner, 85-year-old Sir Tatton Sykes, 5th Baronet, was quietly eating his lunch and looking forward to moving on to his pudding.

Unknown to him, a roof-beam, protruding into the chimney above the Kitchen in the North-East Wing, was smouldering. Steadily, the fire began to spread to other roof-beams and then it really took hold, black smoke billowing across the sky.

For quite some time, the great bell of the Hall was rung to sound the alarm, summoning the help of estate employees: farmhands, grooms, coachmen and just about everyone that was available – even children from the local school.

Sledmere agent, Henry Cholmondeley, ran into the Dining Room to inform Sir Tatton of the calamity but seemingly unimpressed the old man calmly said 'I must finish my pudding, finish my pudding'.

Scene outside Sledmere House during the 1911 fire

The Malton fire brigade, located 12 miles away, sped to the scene as quickly as possible across the difficult terrain in wooden wagons hauled by heavy horses. The Driffield fire brigade were also on their way.

Before any of them arrived, attempts were made to quell the flames by a human chain of villagers passing buckets of water between a reservoir supplying the house. Of course this was useless. Hoses brought by Malton fire brigade captain Jackson, who arrived independently, were attached to fire hydrants near the house and strenuous efforts were made to spray water on flames engulfing the roof at the north east corner. This too was futile.

Sledmere staff and many others desperately try to save priceless objects from the 1911 inferno.

In anxious moments like these there is always someone who finds superhuman strength or guile turning events round or obtaining the best results from a hopeless situation. The person this time was Sledmere agent, Henry Cholmondeley who ordered the human water bucket chain to relocate and salvage as much of value as possible from the burning house.

Reports stated that servants behaved with wonderful pluck and coolness in removing anything that was easily carried such as paintings, glass, china, carpets and furniture; the maidservants 'acting as coolly and bravely as the men'. The fire, however, was now gaining rapid hold and was fanned by a slight breeze, which caused all the upper rooms of the East Wing to blaze fiercely.

The Driffield Brigade, arriving about half past two, were only equipped with a manual engine, and this was quite useless for projecting water to the roof. The Malton brigade, having experienced some difficulty

Sir Tatton Sykes, in foreground, paces around anxiously outside the burning house

with horses, and some very steep hills to climb, reached Sledmere shortly after three o'clock. They immediately got to work in the courtyard at the back of the house and with their steam appliance sent streams of water on to the roof.

Shortly after the arrival of the Driffield Brigade the roof of the East Wing fell in with a loud crash, and this rendered the work of the rescue parties additionally difficult and dangerous.

Sir Richard Sykes

On the lawn outside, strewn as far as the eye could see were priceless antiques of every description. Rare books in the splendid vast Library were hastily thrown outside to eager rescuing hands below.

Having been rudely interrupted from his lunch, Sir Tatton, often described as a rather withdrawn man, walked up and down, with a sullen expression on his face and his arms folded behind his back. He asked if a sculpture, a copy in marble of the famous 'Apollo Belvedere', weighing almost a ton could be saved.

'Scores of hands volunteered to remove the statue', recorded the *Yorkshire Post* and the life size figure was carefully carried outside. Rescuers had a narrow escape in salvaging the valuable collections of books in the historic Library, a blazing beam falling amongst them during the work.

The Library was the repository of most of the treasures. Amongst the pictures there was a portrait, by Romney, of Sir Christopher and Lady Sykes. Another valuable canvas was the portrait group of Sir Mark Masterman-Sykes, his wife, and brother, Tatton, by Sir Thomas Lawrence.

The Drawing Room, a handsome apartment, with exquisitely-painted medallions let into the ceiling, contained, amongst other miniatures, one of Peter the Great, given by himself to Richard Sykes, in recognition of services rendered, and as a mark of esteem, and one of the King of Italy given to the family in 1860. The other treasures comprised rare examples of Sèvres, Dresden and English ware, old Sheffield plate, Venetian brocades, wood carving and much beautiful Hepplewhite, Chippendale, and Louis Seize furniture.

Fortunately, the famous stud at Sledmere escaped any connection with the fire, the stud farm being some distance from the destroyed mansion

At noon the following day, the former house was nothing but a roofless shell and Sir Tatton commented: 'These things will happen, these things will happen'. Nothing remained of the old mansion but the bare walls. Three valuable pictures in the drawing room were burnt; the damage was estimated at around £60,000. Practically everything of value had been saved and many items moved to Sledmere church.

Sledmere House plan of 1751.

The house dated from the late 18th century. In 1751 Sir Richard Sykes (b. 1706) demolished entirely (except for a some ancient brickwork), a medieval gabled mansion and built a new house. No image, if there ever was one, survives of the old property and the encircling landscape was largely devoid of trees.

Sir Richard was from a family of very successful Hull shipping merchants and on inheriting Sledmere from an uncle in 1748, was intent on rebuilding. An entry in his diary states: 'June 17th, 1751 – Laid the first stone of the new house at Sledmere'. Described as being in 'a dramatic Neo-Classical style', the house was built, near the plot of ground where the old house stood, in brick with heavy stone facings. Resembling a property erected in the Queen Anne period it was reached from the local village via two formal avenues.

Between 1749-1750 some 20,000 trees were planted including Beech, Wych Elm and Sycamore. It is believed the new house comprising three storeys and of seven bays was completed by 1753 and Richard Sykes had taken up residence there by the following year. Amongst the interior rooms were eight bedrooms, two Dressing Rooms, a Dining Room, Drawing Room and Study, a Hall with a service area which comprised two Kitchens, Servants Hall, Butler's Pantry, Servants Bedrooms, a Laundry, Dairy, Brew House and extensive cellars.

During Richard's time at Sledmere he spent around £40,000 buying and enclosing land. He was made Sheriff of Hull in 1740, and in 1745 Captain of the Hull Volunteers and High Sheriff of Yorkshire in 1752, he died in 1761.

He left no male heir and on his death the estate passed to his younger brother Sir Mark Sykes (b.

1711). The latter was vicar of Roos, near Hull, and spent much of his time on clerical matters. On three occasions he was selected to represent the Clergy of the East Riding in Convocation. However, he did find time to make money and was once described as 'an artful cunning fellow, ready to take all advantages where he can'. He was created a baronet in 1783 shortly before he died in the same year. During 1776 he had handed over the Sledmere Estate to his son Sir Christopher, 2nd Baronet (b.1749).

Sir Christopher sought advice on a new landscape design from William Kent (c. 1685-1748) and 'Capability', Brown. One of the schemes, probably devised by himself, included demolishing the old village and rebuilding it on the eastern boundary out of view. In an effort to completely transform the landscape he planted several hundred thousand trees.

Like his uncle Richard before him, Sir Christopher spent considerable sums buying and enclosing land. In his lifetime it was estimated he laid out £180,000 on land to enrich the Sledmere estate.

Christopher had married in 1770 Elizabeth Tatton, the daughter of William Tatton Esq, of Wythenshaw in Cheshire. With wife and five children, Sir Christopher moved into the old Sledmere House towards the end of 1783.

Sledmere House, by Thomas Malton

MP for Beverley 1784-90, Sir Christopher Sykes died in 1801 and following on from him was his son Mark Masterman Sykes (b. 1771). He was MP for York 1807-1820 a noted bibliophile, and possessed a major private library, rich in *editiones principes*, books printed before 1500 and Elizabethan poetry.

Mark Sykes was twice married: firstly, to Henrietta, daughter and heiress of Henry Masterman of Settrington, Yorkshire, on which occasion he took the additional name of Masterman. She died in July 1813 but on August 2, 1814 he married Mary Elizabeth, daughter of William Tatton Egerton and sister of Wilbraham Tatton Egerton of Tatton Park.

Sir Christopher, 2nd Baronet and Lady Sykes in 1793 by George Romney

Described as an accomplished amateur architect he considerably improved the house and surrounding landscape which amounted to around 5,000 acres. In making improvements to the house he consulted John Carr and Samuel Wyatt but then produced a scheme of his own including elements from the two other men's proposals. His final design was drawn up by Wyatt and Christopher appointed himself as clerk of works. The project to transform his uncle Richard's house began in 1787 but all major building work did not near completion until 1793.

Amongst the radical changes made to the house were: new ranges added to the north and south ends; the main front was turned round so that it faced south; Nottinghamshire stone was used to encase the entire building; a service court was erected to the north. From 1790, Joseph Rose not only designed and undertook all the decorative plasterwork but also advised on the interior: organising ironwork for the staircase, furniture, upholstery and wallpapers.

Sir Mark Masterman-Sykes, 3rd Baronet

He died without issue at Weymouth in 1823; his wife dying in October 1846. He was succeeded by his brother, Sir Tatton Sykes, 4th Baronet (b. 1772), who became a well known sheep farmer and breeder, and a horse racing patron. He was also a master of fox hounds.

Sir Tatton started work in the office of Farrar & Atkinson of Lincoln's Inn Fields, then became a partner in a banking house at Hull. These, however, were not the tasks that suited him. At 19, he walked from London to Epsom (and back) to see the Derby

– a race he only cared to visit once more. At 21, he drove home from Lincoln (a three days' journey) a half-score of pure Bakewell sheep that were destined to make the fortunes of numerous Yorkshire farmers and breeders. He ran his first horse at Middleham in 1803, won his first race as a gentleman rider in 1805 at Malton, and his last in 1829, when he was 57.

Sir Tatton was 74 in 1846 when he led in William Scott's horse—called after him, Sir Tatton Sykes — a winner of the St. Leger Stakes. His last visit to Doncaster was allegedly in 1862, to see his seventy-sixth St. Leger.

He died in March 1863 and his obituary in the *Hull Packet and East Riding Times* of April 17, 1863 reveals some interesting details: 'Up every morning with daylight, breakfasting on milk and an apple tart, over at his kennels (15 miles off, at Eddlethorpe) as early as his horse could carry him thither; then a day of cheery hunting, or of hedging and ditching among his tenants; now and then stopping to relieve a parish pauper by breaking a few heaps of stones for him, just for a rest, refreshing (pretty commonly) the pauper, but severely abstemious himself, and then on again for other work; brain and muscle relieving each other, and both made perfect so far as practice could do it – such was the routine of his daily existence...The facts of his life, if they could be got

Sir Tatton Sykes leads in the winner of the St Leger Stakes at Doncaster in 1846

together, are more marvellous than most people's romances... In truth he was a missionary in his way and one of an uncommonly rare and useful sort'.

A memorial was erected in his memory and he was succeeded by his only son, also called Sir Tatton Sykes (b.1826) – the unfortunate family member associated with the 1911 fire.

Sir Tatton occupied the office of High Sheriff of Yorkshire in 1869 and he betrayed few characteristics of the average racehorse breeder and none of the

Haymakers on the lawn at Sledmere House in 1888

peculiarities of his father. He had a quiet and retiring disposition and devoted his life to social and ecclesiastical reforms. His father made considerable improvements on the estates, which embraced no fewer than 96 farms, while his son entirely rebuilt and modernised each of the farmhouses, adding covered yards, and improving the farm buildings almost beyond recognition. Sir Tatton was well known as a breeder of Channel Island and Shorthorn cattle, and was a regular exhibitor at most of the principal agricultural shows.

Sadly, Sir Tatton did not enjoy a good relationship with his wife and was forced to issue a notice in a number of national newspapers during December 1896. He was the first man to issue such a notice under the Married Women's Property Act of 1882. The notice stated: I SIR TATTON SYKES, Baronet, of Sledmere in the county of York, and No. 46 Grosvenor Street, in the County of London, hereby give notice that I will NOT be RESPONSIBLE for any DEBTS or ENGAGEMENTS which my wife, LADY JESSICA CHRISTINA SYKES, may contract, whether purporting to be on my behalf or by my authority or otherwise.

Thereafter, Tatton was involved with much litigation with his wife which also involved his son Mark and this had a devastating effect on all concerned.

Speaking after the tragic fire of 1911, Sir Tatton said he intended to rebuild the house at the earliest opportunity. York architect Walter Henry Brierley (1862-1926), an expert on architectural restoration had already been consulted, and he thought there would be no difficulty in reproducing the house in all the features which gave it distinction. Sir Tatton spoke regretfully of the loss of the Library Room, which was the finest apartment in the house, and one of its chief beauties.

Commenting about the fire itself and their efforts to bring it under control, Sir Tatton said the real difficulty was in obtaining an adequate water supply. 'This has always been a difficulty at Sledmere', said the Baronet, 'and we only had the ponds to rely on. How to ensure an adequate reserve of water to cope with an outbreak of fire in the future will be one of the chief problems when we rebuild the house.' The house was insured for £110,000 so there was no lack of funds for rebuilding.

On Sir Tatton's death two years after the fire he was succeeded by his son Lieutenant-Colonel Sir Mark Sykes (b. 1879). Sir Mark was an officer of the 5th Battalion Yorkshire Regiment and served in South Africa in 1902, being mentioned in despatches. He travelled widely in the East, and was the author of *Through Five Turkish Provinces* (1900) and *Five Mansions of the House of Othman* (1909).

Construction workers pose in front of Sledmere House being rebuilt in 1913

He looked forward to the challenge of restoring the house. Brierley wanted the remains of the old house demolished and a new one erected. Sir Mark disagreed, stating 'This is an inartistic and vulgar age. We will build a house that is as little typical of the second decade of the twentieth century as possible'.

In any event, the outer walls were sound and it would be foolish to pull them down and start again. Work on rebuilding Sledmere began early in 1913 and was meticulously overseen by Sir Mark. However, the new house did have slight alterations to the old one when completed during the early part of WWI.

A Turkish Room in the house was designed for Sir Mark by an Armenian artist, David Ohannessian. Inspiration was from one of the sultan's apartments in the Yeni Mosque in Istanbul . The tiles were made in Kutahya, Anatolia in 1913 in Ohannessian's workshop, the Société Ottomane de Faïence.

The children of Sir Mark and Edith Sykes strike a pose for the camera in 1915. They are from l to r: Freya, Richard (later owner of the estate), Christopher, Petsy and Angela. [YP]

Sledmere House Staircase Hall, photographed on August 5, 1967. [YP]

After Mark's death in 1919, Sledmere passed to son Richard 7th Baronet (b. 1905). As he was only 14 years old at this time the Sledmere estate was largely run by his mother Edith and her late husband's cousin, Henry Cholmondeley. Richard struggled in the ensuing years without his father's guidance and, much to the his mother's annoyance gained a reputation as a playboy.

The death of his father and mother (in 1930) meant the Sledmere estate had to lose some 10,000 acres to pay death duties. This situation combined with his extravagances meant that a number of drastic changes had to be put in place by the trustees to avoid financial embarrassment. These included reducing Richard's allowance from £2,000 per annum to £500 and selling the portrait of Sir Christopher and Lady Sykes.

By the end of the 1930s, Sledmere's situation was stabilised, the estate now comprising some 18,000 acres. During WWII, the house was taken over by the Royal Army Medical Corps and Richard became Lieutenant of the 7th Battalion Green Howards. His military life ended in April 1942 when invalided out of the army and he afterwards concentrated on running the estate. He married Virginia Gilliat the daughter of a successful banker, and died in 1978. His son Tatton (b.1943), became 8th Baronet.

Open to the public for much of the week all the year round, Sledmre has much to offer the visitor besides a tour round the historic house and gardens. Activities range from Easter lambing to the festival of spring bulbs and from the dog run fun day to the annual Christmas craft and food fair.

The Library, photographed on March 22, 1965. [YP]

Temple Newsam

The Domesday Book of 1086 notes Newsam under its old English name of Neuhusum meaning 'new houses'. Prior to this, two Anglo-Saxon thanes, Dunstan and Glunier are recorded amongst the earliest owners whilst at the time of the survey and, for some years afterwards, the manor belonged to the Lordship of Pontefract held by Ilbert de Lacy and his sons.

Around 1155, Lord of Pontefract, Henry de Lacy, handed over the manor of Newsam to the Knights Templars in exchange for lands in Nottinghamshire. The Knights Templar or Templars was a Catholic military order founded in 1119 and active from about 1129 to 1312. The organisation created Temple Newsam Preceptory or farmstead, south of the present Temple Newsam house and its main purpose appears to have been sheep farming and the production of wool. The Templars lost the land when the order was dissolved in 1307.

The estate was seized for a short time by the Hospitallers but during 1327 Edward III granted the

Henry Stuart, Lord Darnley

Margaret Douglas, Countess of Lennox

manor Temple Newsam to May the Countess of Pembroke. It is suspected that she built a house at Temple Newsam that may have been similar in design to Pembroke College, Cambridge which she financed. In 1337 Edward gave the manor to Sir John Darcy and his heirs male. When Mary died in 1377 the reversion became operative and the estate passed to Philip, grandson of Sir John Darcy, and other members of the Darcy family.

At the age of 21, Thomas Darcy became owner of Temple Newsam in 1488. In *Temple Newsam House* (1951) it is stated: 'It is now believed, with some supporting evidence, that Thomas Darcy was responsible for some of the building in the present structure. It is possible that he rebuilt or altered an earlier house of which there are no records'.

Darcy was beheaded in 1537, ostensibly for the part he played in the Pilgrimage of Grace and seven years later Henry VIII granted the Temple Newsam manor to his niece Margaret, Countess of Lennox and her husband Matthew Stuart, Earl of Lennox. Their son, Henry, styled Lord Darnley, born and educated at Temple Newsam, married Mary Queen of Scots in 1565. Darnley was assassinated in 1567 and the Temple Newsam estates were confiscated by Elizabeth I.

An inventory, discovered from the time of the Lennox occupation of the house, notes amongst other rooms a Hall, Great Chamber, Gallery and a

Portrait of Ludovic Stewart, 2nd Duke of Lennox

Chapel. In later years the great chamber became the Dining Room and the Chapel a Kitchen.

In 1603, James I awarded Temple Newsam to Ludovic Steward 2nd Duke of Lennox (1574-1624). Two years before he died the Temple Newsam estate was sold to Sir Arthur Ingram (c. 1565-1642) for £12,000.

Born at Thorpe-on-the-Hill, Ingram began humbly as a linen draper in London and in 1604 became Controller of the Customs of the Port of London. He was elected MP for Stafford in 1610 and was appointed Secretary of the Council of the North two years later. Knighted by James I in 1613 he was elected MP for New Romney in 1614.

He had many business interests and was involved in a number of controversies particularly regarding the control of alum mines. In 1619 he built a new mansion on the site of the former Archbishop's Palace at York; served as High Sheriff of Yorkshire in 1620; and was elected MP for Appleby in 1621. At one time he possessed over forty estates, many of them in Yorkshire. He was elected MP for Windsor

Temple Newsam 'birds-eye' view by Johannes Kip and Leonard Knyff

in 1640 and subsequently MP for Callington and died in August 1642.

It is considered that Sir Arthur made extensive alterations to an existing house during his lifetime. Speculation also points to Bernard Dinninghof, who had worked previously for Sir Arthur, making plans for the alterations. They included retaining the central building and remodelling the North and South Wings.

A letter of the Earl of Strafford dated 1636 states: 'Temple Newsam is almost burnt to the ground and household stuff to the value of £4,000 all consumed and lost' though it has been difficult to ascertain whether this information is true.

The granddaughter of Sir Arthur allegedly haunts the house and details are currently on a number of paranormal related websites. Mary Ingram was just 14 years-old when she was accosted by a number of highwaymen whilst returning from a party. The gang grasped a valuable pearl necklace from her neck and she was distraught as it had been given to her as a christening present by Sir Arthur.

Supposedly, the next day she knew nothing of the robbery and searched everywhere for the pearls, not eating and drifting into a breakdown until she died two weeks later. Thus, her restless spirit is said to be still searching for the pearls and the paranormal activity manifests itself in carpets rippling, unexplained creaking noises and sudden drafts of cold air.

An idea of how the house appeared by the end of the 17th century is provided by a spectacular topographical bird's-eye view produced by two Dutchmen Johannes Kip and Leonard Knyff and dated 1699.

Passing down several generations of Ingram family members, the house underwent redevelopment in certain sections of the both the interior and exterior when occupied, from 1736, by Henry Ingram, 7th Viscount Irwin (b. 1691). Around the time of his inheritance he is quoted in a letter as saying the house was badly in need of repair. Amongst his alterations were the conversion of the old Chapel in the basement of the North Wing into a Kitchen; a new entrance on the house's north side; and removing a corridor wall in the North Wing. There was also redecoration carried out in the North and West Wings.

MP for Horsham 1721-1736, Henry married Anne Scarborough, but there were no children from the

The Blue Lady ghost of Temple Newsam is thought to be Lady Mary Ingram, the granddaughter of Sir Arthur Ingram. [YP]

Lord Halifax in Peers' Robes, 1937. [YP]

asked for his thoughts on remodelling the South Wing. His work on transforming the gardens is thought to have been completed in the 1770s but some elements like the series of lakes on the north west side were never undertaken.

During 1778 drawings for the South Wing were made by the Adam brothers and work was carried out in 1796 under the direction of the Viscountess; the 9th Viscount had died in 1778. This was along with his title so now there was no male heir.

The marriage of Charles and Frances produced five daughters and following the Viscountess's death in 1807, the eldest daughter Isabella, now Marchioness of Hertford became the owner of Temple Newsam. Following her death in 1834, she was succeeded by the second of the five sisters Frances, a widow, aged 74, and with her only child dead. When she died in 1841, her nephew, Hugo Charles Meynell inherited the Temple Newsam estate and took the name Meynell Ingram. He died in 1869 and his son Hugo Francis Meynell Ingram succeeded him. In 1868, Hugo Francis entertained the Prince of Wales at Temple Newsam when His Royal Highness visited Leeds for the purpose of opening the National Exhibition of Works of Art. He was elected to represent the new Parliamentary division of West Staffordshire and he died three years later.

His widow Emily who he had married in 1863, was the daughter of Charles Wood, 1st Viscount Halifax and their marriage was childless. After his death she

marriage. On his death the 8th Viscountcy was taken by his brother George who died two years later. The 9th Viscount Irwin, Charles Ingram (b. 1727) married Frances Shepheard and together they sought advice from John Carr about a number of schemes for the house including remodelling the South Front.

The gardens as seen from the bird's eye view by Kip and Knyff were quite formal but in 1762 'Capability' Brown was contracted to remodel them. He was also

Leeds Tercentenary celebrations at Temple Newsam, 1926

Open-cast mining near Temple Newsam, 1975. [YP]

The Darnley Room, rumoured to be the room where the Countess of Lennox gave birth to Henry, Lord Darnley. [YP]

made several alterations to the house including removing the wooden 18th century sash windows with stone mullions and leaded lights; rebuilding the North Porch; installing the Great Oak Staircase; and remodelling the Dining Room.

She was a staunch churchwoman, a supporter of many charities, and built a large church at Hoar Cross, Staffordshire. Towards a new church at Holbeck, Leeds she gave about £30,000. She was Lady of the Manor of Leeds, Osmondthorpe, Halton, and Temple Newsam, and a Lady of Justice of the Order of St John of Jerusalem. She spent some

Springwatch at Temple Newsam. Gary Smith pictured with his Eagle Owl named 'Spooky', 2006. [YP]

of the year yachting in the Mediterranean, but never forgot her obligations to those dependent on her.

Mrs Meynell Ingram died in December, 1904 and Temple Newsam was inherited by her nephew Edward Frederick Lindley Wood, 3rd Viscount Halifax (b.1881). He was the surviving son of her brother Charles, the 2nd Viscount Halifax.

Edward's three older brothers died young, leaving him to his father's fortune and seat in the House of Lords. He was born with a withered left arm, but still enjoyed riding, hunting and shooting. He was a devout Anglo Catholic and later Winston Churchhill would nickname him the 'Holy Fox'. His childhood was mainly divided between two Yorkshire houses, Hickleton Hall and Garrowby Hall.

In 1922 he presented Temple Newsam and the 900 acre park to Leeds City Council along with a number of other gifts. These included many of the Ingram family portraits but most of the remaining contents were dispersed. The Viscount Halifax's idea was that Temple Newsam should be to Leeds,

Yorkshire and the North what Hampton Court is to London and the South. He stated he was unable through the burden of taxation to properly maintain the estate and therefore handed it over to the Corporation of Leeds, which paid him the nominal sum of £35,000 in return. For his generosity he was given the Freedom of the City.

In 1938, Temple Newsam was placed under the same direction as the City Art Gallery and has developed successfully as a museum of the decorative arts. The house has acquired items to augment the permanent collection and been the recipient of a number of donations on permanent or semi-permanent agreements. One of the most significant permanent loans is the Chippendale Society's collection of Chippendale works.

Besides offering much to see and appreciate within the house, the Leeds Council-run Temple Newsam estate currently provides facilities for sports including football, golf, running, cycling, horse-riding and orienteering. It also has a children's play park.

Two annual ticketed concerts in the parkland – 'Party in the Park' and 'Opera in the Park' – were staged on the grassed area which slopes down from the house from July 1994. Respectively they accommodated 70,000 and 50,000 spectators each year but both were cancelled in 2014.

Party in the Park at Temple Newsam, 2011 with Pixie Lott. [YP]

Walton Hall

Charles Waterton bird nesting

The history of Walton Hall, near Wakefield, and its parkland, is perhaps inextricably linked with its most famous former occupant 19th century naturalist Charles Waterton.

One of the western world's first environmentalists he turned Walton Park into a sanctuary for animals and birds.

Charles Waterton could trace his family back to the 12th century and one of his ancestors was Master of the Horse to Henry V; another, Sir Robert, was governor of Pontefract Castle when Richard II was held captive there. After the reformation Waterton's family maintained their faith as Catholics and over many years lost material benefits. However, this situation had eased by the 18th century.

View of Walton Hall

Charles' father Thomas, demolished an Elizabethan manor house and built Walton Hall in a Neo-Classical style during 1767. Containing three storeys with a basement, the rectangular building is plain with no carvings except for a relief sculpture just above the main entrance depicting the Waterton family crest. This depicts an otter with a trout in its mouth.

The house is situated on a small natural island, adjacent to the southern bank of a lake covering 30 acres. An original stone bridge giving access to the manor house was replaced by one constructed from cast-iron.

Encircling the house is a parkland of approx. 300 acres which was never landscaped but has included a Kitchen Garden and stables. The Waterton family

Cast–iron bridge approach to Walton Hall

survived on the income received from leasing out arable land, two farms and a few cottages.

Few Yorkshire men can claim to have lived such an exciting, eventful not to mention eccentric life as Charles Waterton. But, he always hated being labelled an eccentric arguing: 'It is a vulgar calumny. I am the most ordinary, the most commonplace of men'.

That apart, Charles, a thin, tall man, who nearly always dressed in shabby clothes, is mainly remembered for talking to insects, fighting with snakes, riding an alligator, living like a monk, bringing the anaesthetic agent *curare* to Europe, and for his natural history and wildlife protection work. He was boldly described by David Attenborough as 'one of the first people anywhere to recognise not only that the natural world was of great importance but that it needed protection as humanity made more and more demands on it'.

Born on 3 June 1782, Charles was initially tutored at Walton Hall then spent his early school years at a newly-established Catholic school in Tudhoe. Later he attended Lancashire's Stonyhurst College, the celebrated college of the Jesuits. Whilst there, his education was sprinkled with bizarre incidents and pastimes. The school's Jesuit Superior caught him

climbing the towers at the front of the college building and almost at the top, he was ordered to return the way he had gone up. Charles recorded that 'by a mutual understanding, I was considered rat-catcher to the establishment, and also fox-taker. I followed up my calling with great success. The vermin disappeared by the dozen'.

In 1802 he voyaged to Malaga, Spain, staying with his maternal uncles and spent much of the time enjoying himself, bird watching and visiting Cadiz and Gibraltar. But, he left in good time to avoid the 'black vomit'. In 1804 he helped manage his family's sugar plantations, in Georgetown, British Guiana (now Guyana).

Between 1812 and 1824 Charles learned to survive for long periods without a gun in the tropical rain forests of South America. One of his adventures included walking barefoot during the rainy season to Brazil. On a trip to Demerara in 1820, Charles captured a cayman or alligator on the Essequibo River, increasing his ever growing reputation as an eccentric. He commented: 'It was the first and last time I was ever on a cayman's back. Should it be asked how I managed to keep my seat, I would answer, I hunted some years with Lord Darlington's fox-hounds'. He would also tell a tale of how he

The poacher entrapped by Charles Waterton

Charles Waterton

reading Alexander Wilson's *American Ornithology*.

Becoming a skilled taxidermist Charles preserved a number of the animals encountered on his expeditions. His method of taxidermy was unique, soaking the specimens in what he described as a 'sublimate of mercury.' His preserved animals are hollow and lifelike and not 'stuffed'. His importance and uniqueness as one of the significant pioneers in British taxidermy has made him well-known in the wider world.

Some of the taxidermy works bring out his anarchic sense of humour. One famous piece (unfortunately now lost) featured reptiles dressed as famous Englishmen and was titled 'The English Reformation Zoologically Demonstrated.' Another included the upper half of a howler monkey and was modelled to resemble an Amazonian Abominable Snowman. It was simply titled 'The Nondescript', now housed in Wakefield Museum along with a large collection of his work which is on loan from Stonyhurst College.

caught an enormous snake, 'whilst it was taking an afternoon nap'.

Many of his exploits during four eventful journeys are recorded in *Waterton's Wanderings in South America* (1826), which allegedly inspired Charles Darwin and Alfred Russel Wallace. Charles wrote *Essays on Natural History* (three volumes 1838, 1844 and 1857) and also travelled extensively in North America being inspired to visit there in 1824 after

After returning to Walton Hall in the 1820s – his father had died in 1805 and his mother a little later – he became increasingly aware of the destruction to the natural world caused by the profusion of industrial activity happening all around him.

Building a nine-foot-high wall around three miles (5 km) of the estate, he turned it into the world's first wildfowl and nature reserve. He also laid claim to inventing the bird nesting box. Over a period of 30

Charles Waterton mounted on the cayman

years 123 species of birds were recorded by him in Walton Park.

Charles regularly climbed tall trees in Walton Park with great speed to observe a variety of birds – owls, jackdaws and blue tits, who seemingly did not mind his presence. On other occasions he invited lunatics up to the Hall from the local asylum encouraging them to admire his lake with its birds through his telescope.

Inside, Walton Hall was like a museum, crowded with natural history items, his taxidermal creations, strange mementoes from his trips abroad, and classical paintings.

On 11 May 1829, at the age of 47, Charles married 17-year-old Anne Edmonstone the granddaughter of an Arawak Indian. Sadly, Anne Waterton died in April 1830 of puerperal fever, just three weeks after the birth of their son, Edmund. Blaming himself for her death, Charles resolved to serve the rest of his life in 'self-inflicted penance for her soul' and thereafter slept on the bare floor, with a hollowed out block of wood for a pillow and a military cloak for covering.

Besides having a unique relationship with animals and birds Charles was also fearless when it came to reptiles, particularly snakes. An experiment he conducted in Leeds involved comparing the effect of Woorali (*curare*) poison and rattlesnake venom on a number of subjects – rabbits, guinea pigs and pigeons. The Woorali had been brought back from a South American adventure in 1812. During the experiment, it was reported that Charles' 'unprotected hand was within a case, in the midst of the deadly poisonous reptiles, and was as much at home as if he had been leisurely selecting the sweetest bon-bon, instead of the most vigorous rattle-snake'.

Being an early opponent of pollution, Charles fought a long-running court case against the Simpson family, owners of a soapworks, established near his estate in 1839. The emission of poisonous chemicals from the works severely damaged the trees in Walton Park and polluted the lake. Eventually Charles was successful in having the works transferred to another location.

A national park in Alberta, Canada, was named after Charles in 1858 by Thomas Blakiston and is known as Waterton Lakes. Charles died seven years later and his coffin was taken from the Hall to his chosen resting place by barge, in a funeral cortege led by the Bishop of Beverley. It was followed at the lakeside by many local people and reports claim that a flock of birds followed the barge; a linnet also sang as the coffin was being lowered.

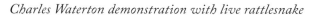

Charles Waterton demonstration with live rattlesnake

Charles Waterton's funeral procession

Edmund, his only heir, sold Walton Hall to family enemies – the Simpsons in 1877 for £114,000. Still existing on an island and accessed only by a pedestrian bridge, the Hall presently forms the main building of a hotel. A Waterton Country Discovery Centre is at the nearby Anglers Country Park at Wintersett.

Catering Students at Walton Hall May 21, 1982. [YP]

Wentworth Castle

Sir Thomas Wentworth (born 1672) must have been distraught on discovering he would not inherit the family fortune and ancestral seat at Wentworth Woodhouse. This was following the death, in 1695, of his cousin the 2nd Earl of Strafford who did not have an heir.

Quite unexpectedly, the inheritance meandered its way down through the female line to the 2nd Earl's sister's son, Thomas Watson. While the latter gentleman adopted the suffix Watson-Wentworth, Sir Thomas Wentworth only gained the title Lord Raby.

Although devastating for Sir Thomas, this unhappy sequence of events seemingly injected him with new life. In 1708 he splashed out £14,150 for Stainborough Hall, which was only six miles from Wentworth Woodhouse and embarked on an ambitious rebuilding programme. Was he devilishly trying his damndest to build a more impressive pile than at Wentworth Woodhouse? Some people firmly believe so and even argue he succeeded.

Stainborough Hall was formerly owned by the Everinghams who, in 1610, sold it to the Cutler family and was bought from the family by Sir

Thomas Wentworth c. 1720

Thomas. As a soldier and diplomat Sir Thomas was a great success, and he was rewarded by two monarchs – William III and Queen Anne. Thus, it was estimated that he had £18,739 tucked away in 1708, to acquire and begin developing Stainborough as a viable Wentworth Woodhouse rival.

Wentworth Castle view of the Baroque east front

Additionally, ownership of the Stainborough estate was essential to the success of Sir Thomas's bid to revive the Earl of Strafford title – extinct from 1695. When this was granted in 1711 he became the 1st Earl of Strafford (2nd creation), much to the chagrin of his rival cousins at Wentworth Woodhouse.

In subsequent years he received handsome salaries from government posts, such as the 1st Lord of the Admiralty and Ambassador to the Dutch Republic in The Hague. This was augmented by a dowry acquired through marriage in 1712 to Ann Johnson, daughter of the shipping magnate Sir Henry Johnson. Inheritances of approximately £51,000 from his wife's family, returns on investments and rents from additional estates, substantially swelled his wealth.

Rebuilt by the Cutler family c. 1672-73, Stainborough Hall (later to become more commonly known as Wentworth Castle) was extended by Sir Thomas, in the Baroque style between 1710-1714. Facing east, the extension was influenced by styles he had seen whilst Ambassador to Prussia and designs were commissioned from architects Jean de Bodt (a.k.a. Johannes von Bodt) and the Swedish Johann Eosander.

The grand building project was supervised by Twickenham architect Edward Reeves. The exterior reliefs were carved by Daniel Harvey, a French mason based in York. Designs for the interiors were supplied by architect James Gibbs from c.1718. The elaborate woodwork was undertaken by Charles Griffiths from London, William Thornton of York and the local craftsman John Goodyear. The decorative plasterwork that commemorates the Peace of Utrecht was executed by Francesco Vassalli and Martino Quadri.

The 180 foot Long Gallery, designed c.1723, emulated precedents in Berlin and Rome and was devoted to sculptures and paintings bought in Italy. The mansion interior was completed with the painting of 'Morpheus and Endymion' by Giacomo Amiconi (1735) in the centre of the Great Hall ceiling.

Royal gardener, George London, designed a series of formal gardens and waterworks, adorned with statues. On the site of an older earthwork, work began, in 1726, building a marvellous miniature medieval castle comprising battlemented gatehouse and bailey wall with four turrets. It is among the first examples of the Gothic folly later to become so

South and East Fronts c. 1900

popular with Georgian landowners. It was visible for miles around and, combined with the inscription 'Rebuilt in 1730', theatrically conveyed the impression that Strafford's family had been on the spot since time immemorial. When completed in 1731, Strafford emphasised his point by giving the folly the ancient name of Stainborough Castle and re-naming Stainborough Hall as Wentworth Castle.

As soon as the son of Thomas Watson-Wentworth, who was also called Thomas, inherited Wentworth Woodhouse in 1723, he launched a cultural counter-attack on Wentworth Castle by lavishly developing his property and re-naming it Wentworth House. A new Baroque front was his first riposte, 1724-28, and from c.1730 a grand Palladian mansion was erected which at 606 feet is considered the longest front of any country house in Britain.

Following Sir Thomas's death in 1739, his son William, (born 1722) continued the rivalry with the Wentworth Woodhouse neighbours and added a Palladian wing to Wentworth Castle. He also embellished the grounds with a swaggering display of theatrical follies.

The design of the Palladian wing, probably by William himself, was tailored to the existing Baroque structure. Although supervised by the London architect, Charles Ross, it is thought to have been built (1760-65) by John Platt of Rotherham, who carved the griffin crest on the pediment (1762) and erected the Corinthian Temple (1764) above the south lawn.

Preferring his country estate to a political career, William transformed the formal avenues and woods of the park into the naturalistic composition of woodland and greenswards, water and monuments so favoured by the English landscape movement.

When William died childless in 1791, the Wentworth Castle estate went through fifteen years of financial hardship which was complicated by the death of three elderly owners in quick succession

After a special Act of Parliament (1795) and acrimonious feuds amongst the families of William's three sisters, Wentworth Castle passed in 1804 to the descendants of the youngest, Lady Harriet. Eventually taking control was, Frederick Vernon-Wentworth (born 1795) who, as a young, committed

Wentworth Castle Gardeners c. 1897.

Wentworth Castle Long Gallery c. 1903.

Woodhouse rivalry both buildings, if not their contents, managed to survive.

To their credit Barnsley Council saved Wentworth Castle and the 60-acre garden in 1948 through a purchase from Captain Vernon-Wentworth for £26,000 (almost twice the sum paid for the estate in 1708). The mansion was converted into a training college for women specialising in nursery and primary school teaching. When the college moved to Sheffield Polytechnic in 1978, Wentworth Castle became the home of the Northern College of Residential Adult Education.

The site was saved between 2003-2013 by the Wentworth Castle Heritage Trust which raised £20m to restore the mansion, gardens, park, home farm, estate church and follies as well as the Great Victorian Conservatory. The first phase was the largest restoration project in the country, enabling the Trust to open the gardens and park to the public in 2007.

man to Wentworth Castle, set about restoring the estate and developing the gardens.

He was succeeded by his son, Thomas Vernon-Wentworth (born 1831), and grandson, Captain Bruce Vernon-Wentworth (born 1862). Thomas installed electricity and built the remarkable conservatory, c.1885. The Captain erected the terrace in front of the Baroque extension (1912) and enclosed it with a new balustrade and ironwork gates with pillars. These were topped with the armorial supporters made c.1720 by John Nost II. Bruce Vernon-Wentworth also replanted the avenue of lime trees known as Lady Lucy's Walk (1919).

Sadly, many of the sumptuous furnishings and furniture were sold off at a sequence of sales in 1911, 1918 and 1948. It would appear that by the 1930s the Vernon-Wentworths preferred their other properties. During the Second World War, the War Office Inventory (1940) recorded a run-down mansion and uncared for lands.

Neglected estates that changed use or witnessed mansions demolished was a sorry event that occurred too frequently and with remarkable alacrity across South Yorkshire and indeed the rest of the country during the first half of the 20th century. Yet, putting aside the old Wentworth Castle and Wentworth

Wentworth Castle Italian staircase.

Italian Staircase, Wentworth Castle Training College.

Wentworth Woodhouse

Wentworth Woodhouse is often described as two 18th century houses merging into one. Yet, the East and West Fronts differ in styles. The west side was completed in 1734, the east side, having the longest frontage in the country – measuring some 606 feet – sometime after 1750. Remnants of an even older house of c. 1630 were incorporated into the west side around 1723. But only a few features still survive.

Sir Thomas Wentworth built the older house. He later became Earl of Strafford, was a minister of Charles I, President of the Council of the North and Lord Deputy of Ireland. But, he made a number of enemies, and was executed in 1641. After him came the 2nd Earl of Strafford and then the estate passed

Charles Watson Wentworth

The east Palladian front of Wentworth Woodhouse. [Author's collection]

The Baroque West Front of Wentworth Woodhouse

to his nephew Thomas Watson. His son, also named Thomas (Watson Wentworth) built the enormous Wentworth Woodhouse known as 'England's greatest semi'.

Henry Flitcroft (1697-1769) was the architect for the Palladian East Front and he also undertook work at Woburn Abbey. The West Front is in the Baroque style and incorporates four giant Corinthian pilasters.

Architectural historian Nickolus Pevsner says of the Wentworth's east and west sides: 'Their centres are nearly, but not entirely, in line, but there is no direct communication around the building. Moreover, there is a considerable difference in level between them which amounts to almost a full storey. The differences in character are even more startling'.

He also states that while the style of the western side is puzzling, it contains motifs which point to south east Germany, and more specifically, Austria and Bohemia.

Thomas Wentworth, Lord Malton and later first Marquis of Rockingham, died in 1750, before the house was completed. From 1715 to 1727, he was MP for Malton, and for Yorkshire from 1727 to 1728. In 1728, he was appointed a Knight of the Bath, admitted to the Privy Council of Ireland in

The Needle's Eye

Hoober Stand

1733 and was Lord Lieutenant of the West Riding of Yorkshire from 1733 to 1750.

Thomas's youngest son Charles, who outlived his four brothers, became the next Marquis of Rockingham. He was also Prime Minister twice and financed the manufacture of Rockingham pottery at the works in Swinton, near Rotherham.

He died in 1782, about the same time that the

house's wings – originally only one and a half storeys high – were altered by John Carr of York. Several other additions to the house as well as a monument (1788) and stables (1768) were also designed by Carr.

On completion Wentworth boasted 250,000 square feet of floor space, 365 rooms (one for every day of the year) and covered an area of over 2.5 acres (1.0 ha). It is surrounded by a 180-acre (73 ha) park and

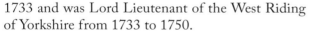

The Doric Lodge

The Stables

Keppel's Column

The Rockingham Monument

by an estate of 15,000 acres.

The rooms of the house include the Pillared Hall, the Painted Drawing Room, the Low Drawing Room, Libraries, Gallery, Chapel, Marble Saloon, the Statuary Room, the State Dining Room, the Yellow Bedroom, Yellow Dressing Room, Anteroom, Van Dyck Room and Whistlejacket Room.

In the Gardens

The most prominent landscape gardener of the time, Humphry Repton (1752-1818), was assigned to lay out the grounds and the work is detailed in his *Some Observations of the Theory and Practice of Landscape Gardening* (1803).

Within the Wentworth Woodhouse Estate are a number of follies/monuments, built during the 18th century satisfying a contemporary craze for that type of feature. These include:

Hoober Stand, a triangular and tapering structure, with a hexagonal lantern extending 518 feet above sea level, was built in 1748 to commemorate the quelling of Jacobite Rebellion in 1745 and the King George II's elevation of Lord Malton to the position of Marquis of Rockingham.

Keppel's Column, a Tuscan structure of 115 feet, is said to never look straight and is named in memory of the acquittal, at his court martial, of Lord Rockingham's friend, Admiral Keppel.

The Needle's Eye, dating from 1780, and lying at the edge of Lee Wood, is the smallest of the four major monuments, and its origins still baffle historians.

Charles Watson-Wentworth, 2nd Marquess of Rockingham died in 1782 and his estates, but not his marquisate, passed to his nephew William Fitzwilliam, 4th Earl Fitzwilliam (b. 1748). He became one of the greatest landowners in the country with the Wentworth estate being made up of approx. 14,000 acres of farm land, woods and mines raising almost £20,000 annually in rents.

William was a prominent Whig politician and served as Lord President of the Council and as Lord-Lieutenant of Ireland

Following his death in 1833, the Wentworth estates and others passed down family members until all the titles became extinct after the death of the 10th Earl, William Thomas George Wentworth-Fitzwilliam (1904-1979).

The house was occupied by the military during WWII and shortly afterwards the 8th Earl, Peter Wentworth-Fitzwilliam was romantically linked with the widowed Kathleen Cavendish, sister of future US President John F. Kennedy. She was killed with Fitzwilliam in an airplane crash in 1948.

The mid 1940s had been marked with the controversial open-cast mining scheme – right on the doorstep of the house – right up to the front

William Fitzwilliam, 4th Earl Fitzwilliam

Peter Wentworth-Fitzwilliam – His first meet, November 7, 1913

— His First "Meet" —
F.L.S.3. Viscount Milton With The Hounds At Wentworth Woodhouse. Nov. 7. 1913.

door. The decision to mine coal in the vicinity was seen as an act of class war against the coal-owning aristocracy. The Minister of Fuel, Manny Shinwell, had carried out a threat to the Fitzwilliams to bring mining 'right up to your bloody front door'.

The scheme was not supported by local miners as the Fitzwilliams were employers known for treating their employees with respect. Although the open-cast mining moved into adjacent fields, the areas that had been affected including the lawns and woods and the renowned formal gardens were not replaced.

At the end of the 1940s, the coal mine-owning Wentworth Estate was greatly affected by the nationalization of the coal industry and death duties. Many of the fine items making up the contents of Wentworth Woodhouse were sold in 1948, 1986 and 1998.

Between 1949-1979, part of the sprawling Wentworth Woodhouse was leased to the West Riding County Council for an educational establishment – the Lady Mabel College of Physical Education, training female education teachers. Forty of the house's rooms, were left as a family apartment.

The college later merged with Sheffield City Polytechnic (now Sheffield Hallam University). By 1988, the Polytechnic no longer required the premises and eventually the family trustees sold them along with a proportion of land. Clifford Newbold, an eminent architect from Highgate, who helped design London's Millbank Tower, eventually acquired the grade 1 property in 1999 and embarked on a programme of restoration. On his death in 2015 it was set to be acquired by Wentworth Woodhouse Preservation Trust.

During the November 2016 budget Conservative Chancellor Philip Hammond announced that the Trust was to receive a grant of £7.6 million 'to help towards urgent repairs to safeguard this key piece of Northern heritage'.

Former students of Lady Mabel College, Wentworth Woodhouse pictured at an annual reunion. [YP]

Lost Yorkshire Country Houses

*Badsworth Hall,
demolished 1940s*

*Alverthorpe Hall,
demolished c. 1945*

*Campsall Hall,
demolished 1980s*

Sprotbrough Hall,
demolished 1920s

Chevet Hall,
demolished 1960s

Methley Hall,
demolished 1960s

*Easthorpe Hall,
destroyed by fire 1960s*

*Horton Hall,
demolished 1960s*

*Kippax Park,
demolished 1950s*

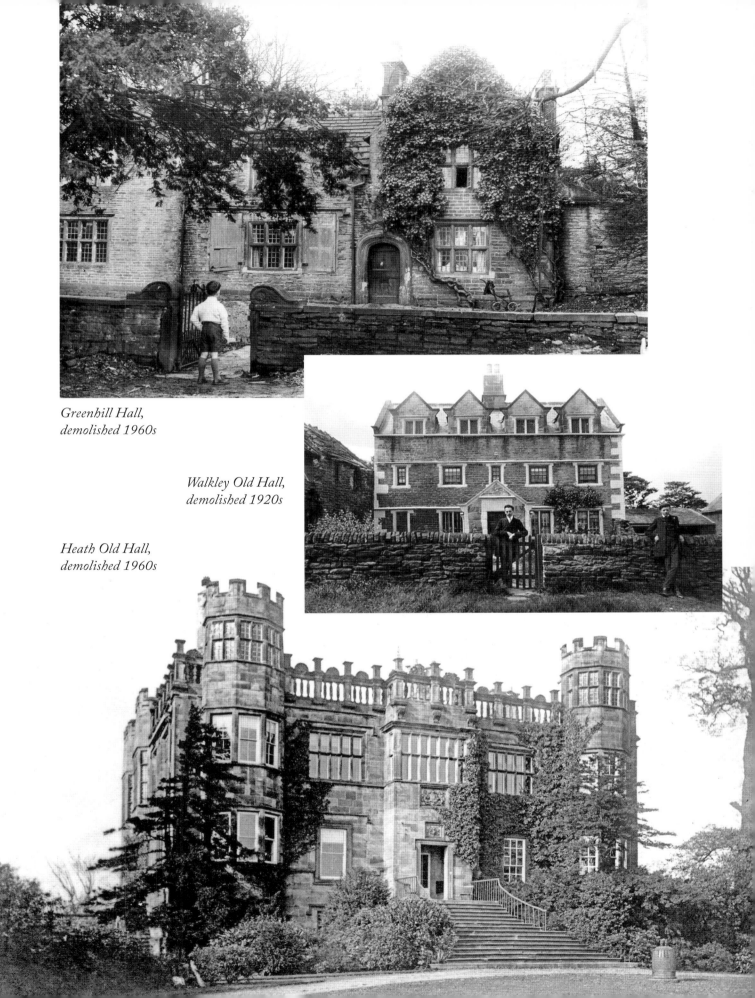

*Greenhill Hall,
demolished 1960s*

*Walkley Old Hall,
demolished 1920s*

*Heath Old Hall,
demolished 1960s*

Bibliography

Burton Agnes Hall & Gardens (2013)

Cannon Hall Museum Park and Gardens The Guidebook (2009)

Carr-Whitworth, Caroline *Brodsworth Hall and Gardens* (2009)

Connell, David *Burton Constable Hall* (2014)

Downes, Kerry *Sir John Vanbrugh A Biography* (1987)

East Riddlesden Hall, Keighley, West Yorkshire. Archaeological Survey Report (2009)

Girouard, *M. Robert Smithson and the Architecture of the Elizabethan Era* (1966)

Hussey, Christopher *English Country Houses Mid Georgian 1760-1800* (1956)

Jenkins, Simon *England's Thousand Best Houses* (2004)

Kipling, Mike *The Gardens at Castle Howard* (2010)

Lotherton Hall (1977)

Morkill, J.W. *The Parish of Malhamdale* (1933)

Morrish, Alison (ed.) *Caring for Cusworth* (n.d.)

Mauchline, Mary *Harewood House* (1974)

National Trust *Beningbrough Hall* (2006)

National Trust *East Riddlesden Hall* (2006)

National Trust *Nostell Priory and Parkland* (2001)

National Trust *Nunnington Hall* (1996)

Neave, David *Sewerby Hall Historical & Architectural Guide* (2008)

Newby Hall (1982)

Radcliffe, Captain Everard *Rudding Park* (1969)

Ripley Castle (n.d)

Robinson, John Martin *A Catalogue of the Architectural Drawings at Carlton Towers, Yorkshire* Architectural History, Vol. 22: 1979

Robinson, John Martin, *Carlton Towers The Yorkshire Home of the Duke of Norfolk* (n.d.)

Saumarez Smith, Charles *The Building of Castle Howard* (1990)

Senior, Janet C. *The Markenfields of Markenfield Hall* (2009)

Sledmere House (1992)

Smith, W.H.Gordon *Cusworth Hall and the Battie-Wrightson Family* (1990)

Sykes, Christopher Simon *The Big House The Story of a Country House and its Family* (2004)

Temple House Leeds (1951)

Wittkower, Rudolf *Palladio and English Palladianism* (1983)

Worsley, Giles *Middlethorpe Hall* Country Life, 12 December 1985